WHO FRA
WILLIAM WEBB ELLIS?

WHO FRAMED WILLIAM WEBB ELLIS?
(...and other puzzles in rugby history)

Tony Collins

Scratching Shed Publishing Ltd

Copyright © Tony Collins 2022
All rights reserved
The moral right of the author has been asserted.
First published by Scratching Shed Publishing Ltd in 2022
Registered in England & Wales No. 6588772.
Registered office:
47 Street Lane, Leeds, West Yorkshire. LS8 1AP
www.scratchingshedpublishing.co.uk
ISBN 978-1739247607

Unless otherwise stated, all photos are public domain
or courtesy of the RFL Archives.

No part of this book may be reproduced or transmitted in any form or by any other means without the written permission of the publisher, except by a reviewer who wishes to quote brief passages in connection with a review written for insertion in a magazine, newspaper or broadcast.

A catalogue record for this book is available
from the British Library.

Typeset in Warnock Pro Semi Bold and Palatino
Printed and bound in the United Kingdom by

TJ BOOKS

Trecerus Industrial Estate, Padstow,
Cornwall PL28 8RW
www.tjbooks.co.uk

Contents

Introduction 1

1. Who Framed William Webb Ellis? 5
2. Why Is Rugby Played With An Odd-Shaped Ball? 11
3. How Rugby Scored The Greatest Own-Goal Of All Time 16
4. League Or Union: Which Is The Real Rugby? 22
5. Why Didn't Soccer Have Its Own 'Great Split'? 27
6. Why Does Wales Play The Wrong Type Of Rugby? 34
7. Why Didn't Lily Parr Play Rugby? 39
8. The Mystery Of Sherlock Holmes's
   Missing Three-Quarter 45
9. Unintended Consequences: How The All Blacks
   Kick-Started Rugby League Down Under 49
10. Did Australian Rugby Union Lose The Code War
    Because It Was Too Patriotic? 54
11. Why The 'First Lions' Weren't The First
    (And Weren't Even Lions) 59
12. Inner City Blues (And Reds):
    How Manchester Was Lost By Rugby 64
13. The Pen Is Mightier Than The Ball?
    How *Tom Brown's School Days* Launched Rugby 70
14. Rugby's Line-Out And Soccer's Throw-In:
    Separated At Birth? 75
15. Are Leicester Tigers The Most Important Club
    In The History Of Rugby Union? 80

16. Who Painted The Players Out Of William Wollen's
    'The Roses Match'? 86
17. Why Scrums Aren't What They Used To Be
    (But Never Were Anyway)? 91
18. Leeds United's Secret Rugby League History 97
19. Why Doesn't Robert Delaunay's Painting
    'The Cardiff Team' Show The Cardiff Team? 103
20. Why Are There So Many Penalty Goals In Rugby Union? ...109
21. Why Does Hull Have Two Professional Rugby Teams? 115
22. Is *This Sporting Life* Really A Film About Rugby? 121
23. When Rugby League Was Almost A Jewish Game 127
24. How Lucius Banks Became America's
    First Pro Rugby Player And Rugby's First Black Pro 133
25. Did Melrose Invent Rugby Sevens? It's Complicated 138
26. How Romanian Rugby Became A Cold War Football 144
27. How Wigan v Bath Showed How Rugby Had Changed
    ... Or Did It? 150
28. 1-2-3-4! The Rise And Fall (And Rise?) Of Drop-Goals 156
29. Imitation Is Not Just A Form Of Flattery:
    Why Union Borrows From League 162
30. The Game That Won't Die: Why Reports Of Rugby
    League's Death Have Been Greatly Exaggerated 168

Introduction

Rugby is full of mysteries. On and off the pitch, the puzzles deepen the more you know about the game. It is played with an odd-shaped ball. There are two versions. The rules seem to change regularly. Fans of the two games still argue about things that happened over a century ago.

In fact, as this book explains, rugby's mysteries go all the way back to its birth. Did a schoolboy called William Webb Ellis really invent the game two hundred years ago in 1823? The truth, as always, is much more interesting than the schoolboy myth.

Such mythology has always been a major feature of rugby history. It emerged during the culture wars which led to rugby's great split of 1895, and has continued ever since. Which game can claim to be the authentic version of rugby? Who can rightly claim the original British Lions? Why did rugby league become the dominant rugby in Australia? How come it isn't the premier code in Wales?

The puzzles extend to what happens on the pitch. Why does rugby union follow football and have a throw-in? What is the role of the drop-goal in the modern age? And what are the reasons for the decline of scrums in both codes? The explanations for these changes in how rugby is played take us way back into the murky past.

One of the most puzzling aspects of rugby history is the fact that the game was once far more popular than football. As you can discover in these pages, Manchester was once a hotbed of rugby, the forerunner of Leeds United was a rugby league club, and football narrowly escaped its own 'great split' in the 1880s. What happened that meant soccer – and not rugby – became the world game?

Even off the pitch, rugby abounds in mysteries.

Would it have become so popular if it hadn't featured in the 19th-century equivalent of Harry Potter, *Tom Brown's School Days*? Why does its most famous work of literature, *This Sporting Life*, seem to dislike rugby so much? What made Arthur Conan Doyle write a Sherlock Holmes detective story about it?

And when it comes to art, were players who switched to rugby league really painted out of a picture about a famous rugby union match? And why doesn't a renowned modernist painting of Cardiff RFC depict the team it is named after?

Who Framed William Webb Ellis? hopes to answer these and many other puzzles. But it is about much more.

Rugby, perhaps more than any other sport, reflects and illuminates the society around it. It divided over the question of social class, its rules developed according to differing ideas about the role of sport in society, and both codes pride themselves on upholding strong, but very different, values. This means many contemporary questions about the game can usually be traced back to an older dispute with roots in deeper questions about the world we live in.

Rugby offers us a unique lens to look at social history –

Introduction

and it reminds us that the past is never over, but continues to reverberate in our present day like ripples in a pond.

Each chapter of this book began life as an episode of my *Rugby Reloaded* podcast, which began in 2018, so you can read each chapter on its own or out of sequence. I've edited and updated each one, and cut out the repetitions which inevitably happen in a long-running series, so this book is both a complement to the podcast and a standalone read in its own right.

The great Australian novelist Thomas Keneally once wrote that rugby league mimicked life, art and war. *Who Framed William Webb Ellis?* aims to explain why this is so.

1.

Who Framed William Webb Ellis?

Rugby – let's leave codes out of it for now – is the only team sport in the world named after a town. Or to be more precise, it is named after a school in that Warwickshire market town. If you've ever been, you can't help but have noticed how the place is dominated by that famous seat of learning, one of the world's most prestigious private schools.

And there stood proudly out front, overlooking the busy A428, is a larger-than-life bronze statue of William Webb Ellis.

Ellis was the pupil who in 1823, so a plaque at the other side of the school tells us ... 'in fine disregard of the rules of football then played' ... picked up the ball in the middle of a football match and ran with it, 'thus originating the distinctive feature of the rugby game'.

It's a story accepted throughout the world, not least by the international governing body of rugby union, World Rugby, who have called their world cup the Webb Ellis Trophy.

There's only one problem with the story – it's not true.

For a start, the statue does not depict William Webb Ellis. It was only erected in 1997 and is a likeness of the sculptor's 13-year-old son. Other than one drawing of him in middle age, we have no idea what Ellis – a clergyman born to a middle-class family in Salford who died, aged 65, in 1872 – actually looked like.

Most importantly, there is absolutely no evidence that Ellis was the first person to pick up a ball and run with it.

The story originated with a former pupil of the school called Matthew Bloxam. He first mentioned Ellis in an article in the school magazine in 1876, and then in 1880, although he also admitted he had not actually seen Ellis do that himself.

Few took any notice of Bloxam's claim until 1895, when the association of former Rugby School pupils, the Old Rugbeian Society, set up a commission of inquiry to discover the origins of the sport. The inquiry couldn't find a single eyewitness. Nor any former pupils who remembered being *told* Ellis had picked up the ball. Despite this, the inquiry declared William Webb Ellis the inventor of Rugby football.

Ellis had been framed. But why?

Let's start by asking: who did actually invent rugby?

The answer is no-one.

For centuries, people around the world have kicked, thrown and carried a ball towards a goal. In almost none of these games were people forbidden from handling the ball, as they are in modern soccer. Just have a look at films of traditional Shrove Tuesday football matches on YouTube to see what many of these games looked like.

In its first few years, even the Football Association allowed players to catch the ball or hit it with their hands. After all, it's as natural to pick up ball with your hands as it is to kick it with your feet. So the basic principles of rugby have existed

Who Framed William Webb Ellis?

as long as people have lined up in two teams and tried to score goals against their opponents.

But when the Old Rugbeian Society met in 1895, the game of football had moved far away from its origins as a traditional folk custom. Britain had two versions – association and rugby football (nicknamed soccer and rugger) – and further major variations were played in Ireland, America, Australia and Canada.

In Britain, both rugby and soccer had become mass spectator sports, played by tens of thousands and followed by millions more. Rugby in the north of England had become the game of the industrial working class. Not only did they make the game their own, they were also very good at it. Indeed, as one former public school boy complained in 1892:

> The majority of Yorkshire fifteens are composed of working men who have only adopted football in recent years, and have no school education in the art, but the majority of members of London clubs have played it all their lives, yet when the two meet there is only one in it – the Yorkshiremen.[1]

The privately-educated leaders of rugby felt they were being swamped by what they called 'working-men players' and would lose control of a game they believed they'd invented.

They had a point. Before 1885, soccer's FA Cup was dominated by teams of privately-educated young men, such as the Old Etonians and Oxford University. Until, in 1885, the FA legalised professionalism. Thereafter, no team of privately-educated players ever again played in the FA Cup final.

Rugby's leaders were horrified at this turn of events, and felt the writing could be on the wall for them too.

So, in 1886, the Rugby Football Union (RFU) declared that rugby would now be a purely amateur sport. Professionalism was outlawed and anyone convicted of receiving money to play rugby would be banned from the game. Harry Garnett, a future president of the RFU, even declared: 'If working men desired to play football, they should pay for it themselves, as they would have to do with any other pastime.'[2]

In response, the northern clubs argued that compensation should be paid to players who lost wages because they took time off work to play rugby, the famous 'broken-time' payments. But the RFU refused any attempt at compromise.

Matters came to a head in 1895 when the northern clubs realised the RFU was going to try and expel them one-by-one. In response, the top northern clubs met at Huddersfield in August 1895, resigned from the RFU, and formed the Northern Union. It was not an accident that this happened in the same year as the William Webb Ellis inquiry took place.

The debate on broken-time was part of a culture war about who rugby belonged to. Those on the side of rugby's leaders declared that the game was the property of the private schools who had nurtured it. England rugby and cricket international Frank Mitchell declared:

> The Rugby game, as its name implies, sprang from our public schools. It has been developed by our leading London clubs and universities; why should we hand it over without a struggle to the hordes of working-men players who would quickly engulf all others?[3]

On the other hand, supporters of working-class rugby players, such as Salford's A.A. Sutherland, argued:

> The prosperity and popularity of the game dates from the time the working man commenced to interest himself in it, both physically and mentally. His success at the game may

Who Framed William Webb Ellis?

not be quite suitable to the tastes of the Corinthian, but it is nevertheless a fact that since he poked his nose into the recreation, football [of both codes] has come on in leaps and bounds.[4]

This wasn't the story rugby's leaders wanted to hear. They needed historical legitimacy to justify their control of the game. Almost all sports — not to mention monarchies, nation-states and political parties – invent their own traditions. These 'origin stories' reflect how administrators see their sport's place in the world. Baseball adopted the myth it was invented by Abner Doubleday, an American war hero, while Australian Rules football likes to imagine it was invented by Aboriginal Australians. There is, of course, no truth to either.

Rugby union was no different. Before 1895, in books like the Reverend Frank Marshall's 1892 classic history, *Football – the Rugby Union Game*, rugby's supporters argued that rugby was the original type of football and that it had been played for centuries by all classes in Britain. The name William Webb Ellis never appeared in histories written at this time.

But the threat of working-class domination of rugby, and the perception that soccer had been taken over by the masses, meant rugby union needed a new creation tale to prove its invention by public schools and so remain their property.

The myth quickly spread across the rugby world, giving historical authority to its leadership and undermining the claims of rugby league to be a legitimate form of the game.

It had one other significant effect. By implying that Ellis was playing a game of soccer when he picked up the ball and ran – despite the fact that the Association code did not come into existence for another forty years – the story also inadvertently promoted the idea that soccer was the original form of football. And by trying to invent a tradition that said rugger had always been the sport of the privately-educated elite, rugby's leaders bolstered the Association code's claims to be the people's game.

So, although it may have helped union to marginalise the working-class influence on rugby, it ultimately allowed soccer – ultimate beneficiaries of the William Webb Ellis myth – to marginalise rugby's place in the history of sport.

Which only goes to show that crime doesn't pay, especially when it comes to history.

---

[1] A Londoner 'Metropolitan Football' in Rev F. Marshall (ed.) *Football – The Rugby Union Game*, (London: 1892) p. 329.
[2] *The Yorkshireman*, 29 Oct 1886.
[3] 'A Crisis in Rugby Football', *St James's Gazette*, 24 Sept 1897.
[4] *Clarion*, 7 Oct 1893.

2.

Why Is Rugby Played With An Odd-Shaped Ball?

One of the most frequently asked questions about rugby is why is it played with an oval ball?

It's a reasonable thing to wonder, soccer being so dominant in most countries we automatically assume a spherical ball is the norm. Yet, as is the case with most aspects of the history of rugby, the story is not quite as straightforward as it seems.

In fact, if we look around the world, five of the seven major football codes – American, Australian, Canadian, rugby league and rugby union – are actually oval ball games. Only soccer and Gaelic football are played with a round ball.

And if we go back to a time before the rules of the modern variations were codified, there were essentially no restrictions on the shape, size, or even type of object that could be used. Usually an inflated pig's bladder did the job, but some games involved other objects. In Leicestershire, in Hallaton's Bottle-Kicking game – as its name suggests – a type of leather bottle was booted about, while in Lincolnshire's Haxey Hood game, a leather tube was used.

There was similar diversity when it came to the different codes of British public school games that shaped our modern incarnations. A Rugby School ball was more oval in shape. The Eton ball was round but much smaller than a soccer ball, whereas the round Winchester ball was much bigger. The Harrow ball is shaped something like a pork pie.

Indeed, balls were not a contentious issue in the early years. The famous 1856 'united' football rules of Cambridge University made no mention of them, despite being written by former pupils of Rugby, Eton, Harrow and Shrewsbury, each of which employed a different shape. Nor was the ball discussed during the Football Association's formation in 1863.

Tradition was a major reason this wide variety of shapes and sizes was accepted. Once a certain type of ball had been introduced, players got used to – and made a virtue of – it.

The other key reason was limitations in manufacturing technology. Before the 1860s, there was no way of producing consistently-shaped inflatable balls. In general, shape was defined by the animal bladder used to make it, so most were neither precisely round nor oval, but looked more like plums of varying size and type. What's more, this also allowed the evolutionary logic of football to slowly emerge.

In the natural world, minor physical differences between animals can give a single species an evolutionary advantage. For example, a species of bird with a slightly sharper beak can flourish because it can dig more worms than a bird with a rounded bill. So too in football, where minor differences in the structure of the ball could give an advantage to players, depending on which rules of football they played.

This explains the popularity of the slightly more oval ball in Rugby School's version. In the 1820s and 1830s, the major

Why Is Rugby Played With An Odd-Shaped Ball?

difference between the Rugby game and the type of football played in other public schools was not whether the ball could be handled, but how a goal was scored.

In all games, you kicked between two posts to score a goal. Some also specified that the ball had to be kicked below a bar or tape across the top of the goalposts. But in Rugby football, it must be kicked *between* the posts and, uniquely, *over* the bar.

This meant balls which gave the kicker more lift became popular as they increased his chances of lifting the ball off the ground. So the more oval it was, the easier a player found it to score a goal by place-kicking or drop-kicking.

Perhaps ironically, given how the rugby codes are today defined as 'handling' games, the evolutionary oval impulse came not from a desire to pick the ball up and throw it about, but to kick it further and with greater accuracy.

The other crucial development factor was the fact that one of England's leading manufacturers of oval balls had its base literally just over the road from Rugby School.

William Gilbert was, according to his own advertisements, a 'Fashionable Boot and Shoe Manufacturer' whose shop was in St Matthew's Street. Gilbert supplied everyday footwear and football boots to the pupils. As with many other cobblers, his expertise in leatherwork led him to expand his business into the production of leather footballs.

He produced these by inflating a pig's bladder, reputedly using his prodigious lung-power, before encasing it in four panels of leather. So popular did they prove that by the mid-1800s Gilbert was Britain's leading ball manufacturer, his wares on display at the Great Exhibition of 1851, Victorian Britain's ostentatious celebration of manufacturing across the British Empire, in London.

Gilbert's display was, in the words of one visitor, 'a house built entirely of leather' showcasing the firm's shoes, boots and footballs, entered in the Exhibition catalogue as 'educational appliances', a nod to the importance football was acquiring in the public schools of the day.

Gilbert's leather panels meant it was partially possible to constrict the shape of the bladder and thereby manufacture balls with greater consistency of structure. Boys from Rugby therefore requested more ovality for better kicking. But it was still impossible to come up with uniformly oval balls, or for that matter round balls for Eton. This would only be possible if pig-bladders could be replaced by a material of guaranteed consistency.

The solution to the problem came from the other side of the Atlantic. In the late 1830s, Charles Goodyear unveiled what he called 'vulcanised rubber', which could be hardened and accurately moulded. Although Goodyear was interested in producing better tyres for motor vehicles, eventually it was realised that vulcanisation could be used to make inflatable bladders for use in sport too – but of exact shapes and sizes.

Yet it wasn't Gilbert who pioneered the rubber bladder in footballs. It was his local rival, Richard Lindon. Lindon may have started his working life as an apprentice at Gilbert's but he soon opened his own shop, also near Rugby School.

He had a strong personal motivation for improving ball manufacture too. His wife Rebecca, mother to his seventeen children, was responsible for blowing up the bladders he used. It was dangerous work with a serious risk of infection and, tragically, she died from a lung disease likely caught from a diseased pig while doing just that.

In 1862, Lindon added to the arrival of vulcanised rubber with his own invention of a brass valve that stopped air being inhaled while the ball was inflated. The modern football had arrived. However, he did not take out patents and so missed the chance to become wealthy from his revolutionary ideas.

Why Is Rugby Played With An Odd-Shaped Ball?

Lindon's technological breakthrough took place at exactly the time when both rugby and soccer were starting to acquire new levels of popularity. The small differences in rules – such as ball shape – now took on much greater importance due to the emergence of organised tournaments between clubs, such as soccer's FA Cup in 1871 or rugby's county cups in the mid-1870s. To play matches in a cup competition meant clubs had to agree on rules, including the shape of the football.

So it was no accident that in the middle of the first FA Cup tournament in 1872 the Football Association first discussed standardising soccer balls. Two weeks before the second FA Cup tournament kicked off, they finally agreed on a size that has remained pretty much the same ever since.

However, it wasn't until 1892 that rugby rules specified the shape and circumference of their ball. Unlike soccer, the RFU refused to allow national cup or league competitions, so there was less pressure for uniformity or precise definitions.

Indeed, debates in rugby about using a round ball were not unusual in the late 19th century, a number of journalists suggesting it would be better soccer-style. Counter-intuitively for us, the discussion was based entirely on the best type for kicking. The supporters of the round ball argued it would be easier for forwards to dribble, while their opponents pointed to greater kicking accuracy with an oval shape.

Shortly after the Northern Union broke from the RFU in 1895, it arranged two experimental matches with round balls. The idea was rejected overwhelmingly, not only because of kicking problems, but also because it made handling and passing more difficult. For an organisation that intended to create the most attractive and exciting form of handling rugby, a spherical 'pill' was shown to be out of the question.

From that moment on, there was never a suggestion that rugby could ever be played with anything but an oval ball.

3.

How Rugby Scored The Greatest Own-Goal Of All Time

If you've ever been to Headingley to watch rugby or cricket you may have driven past the Cardigan Fields entertainment park on Kirkstall Road. Ten minutes from the stadium and opposite the famous Cardigan Arms pub, it's packed with the usual identikit food chains, gyms, bowling alley and cinema.

But 130 years ago, Cardigan Fields was the place to watch state of the art rugby played in front of some of the biggest crowds that had so far been seen in rugby or soccer.

From 1880 to 1889, every Yorkshire Cup final apart from one was played here, attracting five-figure crowds that eclipsed soccer attendances and often outstripped those at the FA Cup final.

In fact, up until the mid-1880s, soccer played second fiddle to rugby right across Britain. Manchester, Liverpool and even the north-east, around Newcastle, were seen as strongholds of the rugby game.

How Rugby Scored The Greatest Own Goal Of All Time

So what happened? How did soccer eclipse rugby? The explanation could well be called the story of rugby's great own goal.

Strange as it appears in the 21st century, at one point in British sporting history rugby was bigger than soccer. When the Rugby Football Union was founded in January 1871, *Bell's Life*, Britain's leading sports weekly, wrote: '...every year has increased the superiority in point of numbers and popularity of the rugby clubs over those who are subject to the rule of the [Football] Association.'[1]

The newspaper saw no reason why rugby's place as the premier winter sport would not continue. After all, at the Football Association's annual general meeting in 1870 – seven years after it was founded – the FA had just 26 adult clubs in membership. In contrast, the RFU had 20 adult clubs at its very first meeting a few months later.

And by the time the 1874-75 season kicked off it had one hundred and thirteen clubs under its banner. The FA had only 78. A decade later in 1880, *The Times* pointed out that 'the players of the rugby union game are probably twice as numerous as those of the Football [Association].'[2]

But in 1871, the seeds of change were being sown. The FA decided to launch a knock-out cup competition, the FA Cup, and over the course of the next decade, the FA Cup became the catalyst for soccer to expand.

At this time football had no leagues and all matches were friendlies, so the Cup gave teams something to play for and increasingly became the focus for local rivalries. What's more, teams from opposite ends of the country could now play each other. And, as the sport spread across society, working-class teams could play sides comprised of the British elite.

The most famous example of this took place in 1878, when Lancashire mill-town club Darwen played Old Etonians in the quarter-final stage. They drew 5-5, and then 2-2, before Darwen finally succumbed 6-2 to the ex-public schoolboys. It was a match that captured the national imagination, not only due to its epic nature, but also for pitting representatives of the British ruling class against representatives of northern textile workers. It would have been impossible for men from these two classes to meet on equal terms in any other sphere of British life. The match gave soccer a social meaning that resonated far beyond a simple contest for a sporting trophy.

But the RFU refused to organise a rugby version of the FA Cup, despite support for the idea within rugby. In 1876, the Royal Military Academy at Woolwich offered a cup to the RFU for a national knock-out competition, but was turned down.

More famously, in 1878 the recently disbanded Calcutta rugby club gave the the RFU 'a challenge cup to be annually competed for by all rugby union clubs'. The RFU wrote back explaining the 'difficulties of all clubs playing together' and instead the trophy found fame as the Calcutta Cup for the England versus Scotland match.

This obstinacy was defended by RFU secretary Rowland Hill, who argued: '...we again venture to enter our earnest protest against challenge cup competitions. Why are they continued? It is said that they aid materially in increasing an interest in the game. Rugby Football requires no such unhealthy stimulants.'[3]

The fundamental problem was that RFU leaders disliked how cup competitions meant that you couldn't choose your opponents. In the 1870s, the *Sporting Gazette* even published lists of those which could be considered 'Gentlemen's Clubs', to enable its readership to avoid playing 'socially-inferior' sides by accident. But in a knock-out competition, ones opponents were literally down to the luck of the draw.[4]

How Rugby Scored The Greatest Own Goal Of All Time

Rugby's refusal to stage a national cup tournament gave soccer a huge advantage as the two codes battled for new supporters. And the consequences of the RFU's head-in-the-sand approach were clear to many rugby supporters. In 1884, a letter to the weekly *The Field* argued that 'unless a Rugby Union Challenge Cup be speedily established, in a few years the Association clubs throughout the kingdom will outnumber those of their rivals by at least ten to one.'[5]

The failure of the RFU to take heed was most damaging in Lancashire. Here, with the exception of some of the East Lancashire mill towns, soccer played second fiddle to rugby until the late 1870s. But the success of local Lancashire soccer cups and leagues eroded rugby's position. The refusal of the Lancashire RFU to organise a county-wide rugby cup tournament like rugby's Yorkshire Cup, which had begun in 1877, meant that cities such as Liverpool and Manchester, formerly strongholds of the rugby code, were gradually colonised by soccer. The scale of the swing from rugby to soccer can be gauged by the fact Burnley and Preston North End were both rugby teams until the early 1880s.

Soccer underwent a huge expansion at that point due to the success of Lancashire clubs in the FA Cup, which brought national fame to such as Blackburn Olympic, who became the first northern professional side to win the Cup in 1883.

The legalisation of professionalism by the FA in 1885 and the formation of the Football League in 1888 gave soccer a prominence and competitive structure that undermined rugby's national appeal even more.

In fact, there was a significant body of opinion in rugby which actually welcomed the rise of soccer. 'The loss of followers to the grand old game [of rugby] is regrettable,' wrote one supporter of the RFU's strict amateurism in the 1889 *Football Annual*, 'yet looking at the present state of all professional sports we cannot but think that this possible loss is far preferable to legalising professionalism.'

Soccer was also helped by the civil war that broke out over the RFU's 1886 amateur rules. Rugby players and clubs were suspended for breaking anti-professional regulations and the increasingly chaotic organisation of rugby contrasted sharply with the efficiency of the Football League. Public perceptions of rugby as a fractured sport at war with itself did nothing to help it win new supporters or players.

Although it seems odd now, the truth was that the majority of rugby's leaders did not want to popularise the game. For them, rugby was a sport for moral education and physical recreation, not to be merely watched. The commercialism and crowds of soccer and northern rugby were an abomination. 'The football players of the future will be compelled to forget the honourable traditions of this great English game, and to pander to the howling mob that crowd the circular stands of some Yorkshire coliseum,' warned Bertram Robinson in 1895.[6]

Not to be outdone, the journalist Glyn Roberts explained a few years later how: 'I visit a soccer match once a season to keep my disgust fresh', a sentiment that appears to have been widespread, if rarely expressed quite so sharply.

The consequences of this attitude quickly became clear. Just over a decade after rugby's 1895 split, the Football Association had over 7,500 affiliated clubs, roughly fifteen times the number of all rugby clubs in the RFU and Northern Union combined.

Hindsight is a wonderful thing, but it doesn't take much imagination to see that if the RFU had accepted the offer of a cup from the Calcutta Club in 1878, rugby could perhaps have consolidated its dominance of the winter sports scene. The national popularity the FA Cup brought to soccer might have been thwarted. Cup finals between the leading northern

How Rugby Scored The Greatest Own Goal Of All Time

teams like Wakefield or Wigan and the elite middle-class clubs such as Blackheath or Richmond in the south would have captured the wider imagination. And rugby would have remained the dominant national winter sport of Britain.

And who knows how that would have impacted on the development of association football around the world in the 20th century?

The RFU's refusal to create rugby's own version of the FA Cup may well have been the greatest own goal in the history of British sport.

---

[1] *Bell's Life* in London, 7 Jan 1871.
[2] *The Times*, 12 Nov 1880.
[3] 'The Past Season', in C.W. Alcock (ed.), *Football Annual* (London: 1883) p. 17.
[4] *Sporting Gazette*, 28 Dec 1872.
[5] *The Field*, 12 Jan 1884.
[6] B.F. Robinson, *Rugby Football* (London, 1896) p. 55.

4.

League Or Union: Which Is The Real Rugby?

Although nowadays we think of league rules having little in common with union rules – people sometimes say the only similarity is the shape of the ball and the posts – the roots of rugby league can be traced back to the debates about rugby rules which took place long before the game split in two.

In fact, just as much as rugby union, rugby league rules evolved from the game played by all rugby clubs before the creation of the Northern Union in 1895.

Rugby union rules are the road rejected by the northern rugby clubs who created rugby league, while rugby league rules are the road not travelled by rugby union. Both are variations of rugby as played in the 1870s, 1880s and 1890s.

The original rules of rugby looked nothing like modern rugby union or rugby league. The first rules of the Rugby Football Union of 1871 specified that teams were twenty-a-side, usually comprising two full-backs, two half-backs, one

League Or Union: Which Is The Real Rugby?

three-quarter, and fifteen forwards. As you can guess from that latter number, the scrum was the most important feature of early rugby and the focal point of the action.

Prominent RFU official and player Arthur Guillemard described how the early scrum worked. As soon as the ball-carrying player was brought to the ground with a tackle, he stood up as both sets of forwards gathered around him and 'directly the holder of the ball has succeeded in forcing it down to the ground, he shouts "Down" and [the] business [of the scrum] may be commenced at once.'[1]

In complete contrast to today, the aim of the scrum was not to heel the ball out, but to drive the ball forward and break up the opposing pack, so scrums would often last for minutes while both sets of forwards tried to dominate. Passing the ball was extremely rare.

The centrality of the scrum in early rugby inevitably led to problems. To solve this, teams were reduced to fifteen-a-side. Scrums no longer lasted for minutes at a time, because it was easier for the ball to come out. Most importantly, to the horror of traditionalists, teams began deliberately to heel the ball out of the scrum to the backs.

Fifteen-a-side also opened the way for the development of a passing game. The speed with which the ball left the scrum now offered a quick-thinking half-back the chance to move the ball quickly to his three-quarters or loose forward. In 1878 the rules were changed again to make the ball-carrier release the ball immediately the tackle was completed, speeding the scrum up even more.

Innovation quickly followed in those areas where rugby had become a mass spectator sport. In South Wales, Cardiff introduced the four three-quarter system in the mid-1880s, and in the north of England, the popularity of the Yorkshire Cup propelled the game to new levels of sophistication.

When a team from the mining village of Thornes, near Wakefield, won the Yorkshire Cup in 1882, they did it using a wing-forward to protect the scrum-half, and for the first time allocated specialist positions to forwards in the scrum and line-out.

Originally in rugby only goals counted in the score – a try was precisely that, it allowed the scorer to try and kick a goal, but a try on its own scored no points. However, the increasing importance, and spectator appeal, of try-scoring led in 1886 to the RFU awarding one point for a try and three for a goal. But this recognition of a try's value was undermined three years later when penalty goals were awarded two points. By 1895, three points were awarded for a try, the same number as for a penalty goal.

But for most spectators, especially in the North of England and South Wales, the passing game and scoring of tries were the essence of rugby. One Yorkshire journalist argued: 'A try in the vast majority of instances is the most deserving point in the game, and calls for the greatest exertion on the part of the team as a whole. On the other hand, the responsibility of placing a goal is an individual responsibility.'[2]

The huge growth of soccer in the 1880s also meant rugby had to compete as a spectacle by promoting tries over goals and reducing the number of scrums and line-outs. In 1892, three years before the 1895 split, James Miller of the Yorkshire Rugby Union praised rugby's move to fifteen-a-side in the 1870s but argued it was time to take another step forward: 'The game has now reached a period when another radical change must be considered, and that is the reduction of players from fifteen to thirteen.'[3]

So even before the creation of the Northern Union in 1895, an alternative roadmap for the future was being laid out.

A fortnight after the famous meeting at Huddersfield's

League Or Union: Which Is The Real Rugby?

George Hotel which created the Northern Union in 1895, Halifax and Leeds proposed moving to thirteen-a-side teams. Leeds committee member Harry Sewell, argued: 'We want to do away with that scrummaging, pushing and thrusting game, which is not rugby, and that is why I propose to abolish the line-out and reduce the number of forwards to six. The rugby public does not pay to see a lot of scrummaging.'

Shortly after, in December 1895, Halifax's Joe Nicholl proposed that: 'The Rugby game of football as played by the Northern Rugby Football Union should be played by thirteen players on each side, and to consist of six forwards, two half backs, four three-quarters and one full-back.' His proposal lost by eighteen votes to nine, and the Northern Union continued to be a fifteen-a-side game.

The NU's failure to change with the times cost it dearly over the next decade. At the end of the first season, there were worries about the lack of tries scored, so in 1897 the value of all goals was reduced to two points, one point fewer than a try, placing the emphasis firmly on the scoring of tries.

The line-out was also abolished in 1897 because, as one NU supporter explained: 'It is an unattractive incident succeeded by a scrummage, [and] a piece of play which is undesirable in a scientific and sportsmanlike sense.'[4]

In 1899, the NU decided to get rid of the traditional rugby union ruck or maul after a tackle by introducing a rule that, when a tackled player could not release the ball, a scrum had to be formed. But many in the NU still thought the problem was caused by too many forwards on the pitch.

In 1903, NU clubs voted fifty-four to twenty-four to make it a twelve-a-side game. The motion failed by just five votes to get the three-quarters majority necessary to go into the rule book. Even so, by the start of the 1904-05 season, virtually every non-professional NU competition played twelve-a-side.

Who Framed William Webb Ellis?

This left the NU in limbo. Eventually the issue came up again at the 1906 NU annual meeting. Bradford wanted to go back to RFU rules. Whitehaven Recreation wanted twelve-a-side. Warrington and Leigh proposed thirteen-a-side, while St Helens even suggested fourteen-a-side. Finally, after a decade of indecision, thirteen-a-side was adopted by forty-three votes to eighteen.

To solve the problem of endless scrummaging, the meeting also voted to introduce a new rule about the tackle. Instead of a scrum being formed, the tackled player got to his feet, put the ball down and played it with his foot, usually to a team-mate standing behind him.

This was seen as a version of the original rugby union scrum rule, whereby the tackled player had to stand up with the ball, wait for the scrum to gather around him and then put the ball down on the ground and play it with his foot. The play-the-ball had been born.. by talking a half-step back to the rugby rules of thirty years before.

The adoption of thirteen-a-side and a play-the-ball marked the final break with the RFU's conception of how rugby should be played. Three decades of debate had finally led to the rules of modern rugby league and the underlying philosophy of the game, which remains at its heart to this day, as neatly expressed by Hull chairman Charles Simpson: 'The essence of our existence is a game without monotony.'[5]

So which is the real rugby? Neither. Or both.

Real rugby, like beauty, is in the eye of the beholder.

---

[1] 'The Rugby Union Game With Hints to Players', in Thomas P. Power (ed.) *The Footballer* (Melbourne: 1877), p. 11.
[2] *The Yorkshireman*, 4 April 1893.
[3] *Yorkshire Post*, 9 Oct 1892.
[4] *The Yorkshireman*, 19 Oct 1895.
[5] *Yorkshire Post*, 30 May 1903.

5.

Why Didn't Soccer Have Its Own 'Great Split'?

Picture the scene. A sport's national governing body tries to crack down on players being paid. Northern clubs rise up in rebellion. The game is gripped by controversy and dissent, which take it to verge of a split.

But this isn't rugby in 1895. It's soccer in 1885.

One of the most fascinating questions in the history of modern sport is why did rugby football split over the question of payments to players in 1895, but soccer stay united when, ten years earlier, it introduced payments to players.

The answer has a lot to do with timing.

In the late 1870s, knock-out cup competitions in soccer and rugby across the North of England became hugely popular. These tournaments turned the game into much more than a few people chasing a ball around a field. Winning cups, not to mention defeating local rivals, brought fame to clubs and glory to towns. Football of whichever code now had a wider social importance, giving clubs an incentive to seek out players who could build a winning team for their communities, regardless of where an individual player might come from. And attracting the best players often meant paying them or providing a job, sometimes both.

Not only that, but knock-out tournaments also meant clubs could no longer choose their opponents, undermining the social aspect of the game so important for gentlemen's football teams. As we've seen, thanks to the draw for a knockout cup, a gentleman's club could find itself competing against a side it considered to be socially inferior. Most importantly, it might even lose to them, as the Old Etonians almost did to Darwen in 1878. Cup competitions therefore tended to undermine the social etiquette that had previously governed the sport.

Underlying these fears was social snobbery and a desire to use fixtures to maintain the status quo between the classes.

This was true throughout British sport. In 1861, the *Rowing Almanack* excluded 'tradesmen, labourers, artisans or working mechanics' from events under its jurisdiction. Shortly after, the Amateur Athletic Club, the forerunner of the Amateur Athletic Association, also barred anyone who was 'a mechanic, artisan or labourer' from membership.[1] Rowing and athletics had long traditions of working-class involvement and it was the need to make sure that lower-class athletes did not threaten upper- and middle-class control that led to such open class prejudice.

So when the first reports of players being paid or offered employment to play soccer and rugby appeared in the late 1870s, the leaders of the Football Association and the Rugby Football Union felt something had to be done.

Initially, soccer's leaders were actually more determined

Why Didn't Soccer Have It's Own 'Great Split'?

to fight professionalism than the RFU, which did not seriously debate the issue until 1886. But in soccer there were numerous discussions about how to combat professionalism. As early as 1882 the FA decided that any player who received more than purely his expenses to travel to a match 'shall be debarred from taking part in either cup, inter-Association or International contests and any club employing such a player shall be excluded from this Association'. Interestingly, the FA included 'any wages actually lost by any such player taking part in any match' – what became known as 'broken-time payments' – as legitimate expenses.[2]

But it was already too little, too late.

Barely eighteen months after this decision, the issue came to a head when Upton Park, a London gentlemen's club, drew 1-1 with Preston North End in the fourth round of the FA Cup. Upton Park appealed against the result, claiming that Preston had fielded players who had been paid to come from Scotland to play for them and who were receiving more than their expenses to play, contrary to the 1882 resolution. When confronted with the evidence, Preston secretary William Sudell cheerfully admitted that the club found jobs for its players and that this was standard practice among Lancashire clubs.

The class snobbery that lay behind the dispute was illustrated by the *Preston Guardian*, which pointed out that the club's players were paid because 'no working man can be an amateur football player.' Preston were suspended from the FA but, seeing the chaos that would ensue if every club which paid its players was suspended, FA secretary Charles Alcock proposed legalising professionalism on the same basis as in cricket.

Alcock's was at first a minority view so the FA's assistant secretary N.L. Jackson (who would become famous as the secretary of Corinthians FC) suggested setting up a committee to look into the issue. It reported back in June 1884 and recommended that players who took time off work to play should be paid 'broken-time payments', but that all other forms of payment should be banned. Clubs which broke the law would be expelled from the FA. To curb the number of Scots players in Lancashire – derogatorily called 'Scotch Professors' by English journalists – it was also proposed only English players should be allowed to play in the FA Cup.

This was not acceptable in Lancashire. Galvanised by Preston's suspension, the county's top clubs met and decided that 'a northern association be formed which will promote the interest of football generally in the northern districts.' When the FA then announced clubs would be banned from the FA Cup if they fielded, or played against a club fielding, an ineligible imported player, seventeen northern clubs met to form the British Football Association (BFA) in October 1884. The following week the BFA invited soccer clubs to a meeting in Manchester to 'promote and consolidate a powerful organisation which will embrace clubs and players of every nationality'. Seventy delegates representing thirty-seven clubs attended the first national British Association meeting. A football split was on the horizon.

The northern clubs behind the British Football Association viewed the new FA rules as a deadly threat. If they could not play against clubs with 'imported' players, their fixture lists would shrivel and their revenues quickly dry up. For the top clubs, football had become a commercial business and the loss of attractive fixtures would bring financial ruin. Amateurism was not compatible with the mass spectator sport which soccer had now become.

Faced with the imminent threat of a new, rival association, the FA started to back-track. Four days after the British

Why Didn't Soccer Have It's Own 'Great Split'?

Association meeting, the FA suspended its proposed ban on imported players and called a special general meeting to discuss professionalism. Eight days later, it decided that it was 'now expedient to legalise professionalism under stringent conditions.' But many in the FA still opposed any compromise with professionalism and it took three special conferences of the FA before, on 20 July 1885, professionalism was finally legalised. Football's great split had been avoided.

Nevertheless, professional players were very strictly controlled by the FA. All professionals had to be registered by the FA, they could not change clubs without permission of their club and the FA, and they were subject to a residential qualification before they could play in the FA Cup. Nor could professionals sit on any FA committees. In short, players would be paid to play football, and play was all that they would be allowed to do.

But if professionalism removed any danger of working-class professional players taking control of soccer off the field, it meant precisely the opposite on the pitch.

Up to 1885, the only teams from industrial towns which had appeared in the FA Cup final were Blackburn Rovers and local rivals Blackburn Olympic. The Cup was dominated by socially-elite teams like the Old Etonians and the Royal Engineers. In April 1885 Queen's Park lost 2-0 to Blackburn Rovers in that season's FA Cup final. It was the last time an amateur gentleman's club would play in it. The following year the Swifts club became the last amateur club ever to appear in the semi-finals. The age of the professional soccer player had arrived, and there would be no turning back.

It did not take long for supporters of amateurism to realise their mistake. The eclipse of gentlemen's clubs by working-class professionals in the FA Cup was their worst fear. Barely two years later, the RFU's Arthur Budd, who became rugby union president in 1888, said: 'Gentlemen who play football once a week as a pastime will find themselves no match for men who give up their whole time and abilities to it... One by one, as they find themselves outclassed, they will desert the game and leave the field to professionals.'[3]

It was soccer's short experience with professionalism which caused rugby's leaders to ban all forms of payment or other rewards to players at its 1886 annual general meeting. Rugby union became a strictly amateur sport and any person or club violating its grandiosely titled 'Laws As To Professionalism' would be banned from the sport.

The stridency of the language used by supporters of amateurism reflected a rising sense of panic among gentlemen footballers of both codes about the consequences of professionalism. Many came to deeply regret the decision to allow players to be paid. N.L. Jackson, who had seconded Charles Alcock's motion that the FA legalise professionalism, changed his mind to become an advocate of uncompromising amateurism. In the 1890s, he would be one of the main opponents of the northern rugby clubs' call for broken-time payments.

In soccer, the social divide between middle-class sides and working-class clubs, whether professional or amateur, became an unbridgeable gulf. Soccer was played by all classes, but after 1885 they almost never played it together.

So soccer was able to remain a united sport but rugby split in two. By legalising professionalism the Football Association avoided its own northern breakaway. But the unforeseen consequence was that soccer became dominated by working-class professional players.

When faced with exactly the same challenge eighteen months later, Rugby Union's leaders learned from what they saw as the FA's mistake and, to stop rugby going down the

Why Didn't Soccer Have It's Own 'Great Split'?

same path, took the opposite course and banned all forms of payments to players.

It was a fateful decision that led to rugby tearing itself apart and leaving the way clear for soccer to become the most popular sport on the planet.

---

[1] For a selection of different sports' exclusionary amateur regulations, the the appendices to Wray Vamplew's *Pay Up and Play the Game: Professional Sport in Britain, 1875–1914* (Cambridge: 1988).

[2] The full story of soccer's move to professionalism (from which this and following quotes are taken) is in Dave Russell's 'From Evil to Expedient: The Legalization of Professionalism in English Football, 1884–85' in Stephen Wagg (ed.) *Myths and Milestones in the History of Sport* (London: 2011) pp. 32-56.

[3] 'The Rugby Union Game' in C.W. Alcock (ed.), *Football Annual* (London: 1886), p. 52.

6.

Why Does Wales Play The Wrong Type Of Rugby?

When I was a boy in the early 1970s, my dad and I would watch what was then called the Five Nations on *Grandstand*, the BBC's Saturday afternoon sports show.

What was going on, I wondered? Why was the ball kicked to touch so often? Why did they let it go when tackled? And why was the home country of some of my rugby league favourites, superstars like Clive Sullivan, Colin Dixon and David Watkins, devoted to such strange rules?

It seemed that Wales was playing the wrong type of rugby.

Much as it has annoyed many of my Welsh friends over the years, I've never escaped the feeling that they are at the wrong game.

After all, if you are from Blaina or Batley, rugby is a working-class sport that became a symbol of the industrial world of mines, docks and factories. Surely Wales should be not be kow-towing to their southern English rulers?

Why Does Wales Play The Wrong Type of Rugby?

It's a question many have pondered over the decades. As soon as rugby became popular in the 1880s, it was clear that Welsh rugby had more in common with northern England than any other region. And although started by the privately-educated middle-classes, just as in Lancashire and Yorkshire, it soon captured the imagination of workers flocking to the towns and villages of South Wales at the end of the century.

There was a natural bond. Both took to the rugby field in an innovative, attacking spirit. The Welsh invented the four three-quarter system; Yorkshire sides introduced tactical innovations like defined forward positions, 'wing-forward' play and passing moves from scrums. Links were quickly cemented on and off the field.

In 1884, Wakefield Trinity, Batley, Dewsbury and Hull visited Cardiff, Llanelli, Neath and Newport. Incoming sides from the north met with outpourings of civic celebration. When Hull arrived at Llanelli railway station in the 1880s, for example, a huge crowd led them on a parade through the town, torchlit by blazing bundles of cotton waste.

And, just as in the north, men used to working five and a half days a week in a mine or steelworks believed hard work deserved financial reward, on or off the pitch. Although the leaders of Welsh rugby supported the RFU's imposition of amateurism in 1886, their clubs were already secretly paying players. Swansea and Wales winger Bill McCutcheon, who went north to play for Oldham in 1888, later admitted that pound notes would mysteriously appear in players' boots.

But in northern England, crowds were bigger and rewards more lucrative for an ambitious sportsman. The first Welsh player known to have 'Gone North', as it became known, seems to have been Llanelli's international full-back Harry Bowen, who signed for Dewsbury in 1884 but returned home after only a handful of appearances.

The first to make a real impact was Cardiff and Wales half-back 'Buller' Stadden who, along with team-mate Angus Stuart, went to Dewsbury in September 1886. Stadden told the *Yorkshire Post* that they were unemployed in Cardiff so 'having made a few friends during Dewsbury's tour of the Principality, they naturally steered for Yorkshire and got employment and a place in the Dewsbury team.'[1]

Luckily, Stadden would have journalists believe, they had both been able to find jobs at a wool spinning factory in the town, Newsome, Sons & Spedding. It was, of course, sheer coincidence that Mark Newsome, one of the sons in the company title, happened also to be the president and former captain of Dewsbury rugby club.

Across the Pennines, Oldham set the pace by signing Bill McCutcheon in 1888, swiftly followed by fellow international Dai Gwyn. Perhaps the most famous such signings were the brilliant brothers, David and Evan James, who transferred from Swansea to Manchester's Broughton Rangers in 1892 for a reputed signing-on fee of £250, in flagrant violation of the RFU's amateur regulations.

Some Welsh players even advertised openly in northern newspapers: 'General Clerk requires a situation, knowledge of French; highest references; wing-three-quarter Welsh team', read an advertisement in the *Yorkshire Post* in 1893.

Welsh clubs responded to the loss of talent to the north by offering inflated expenses and attractive jobs. For some, the business networks of leading Welsh clubs offered greater opportunities for social mobility, a perk northern clubs could not match. But the desire of working-class players to be paid, and the ability of Yorkshire and Lancashire sides to pay them, ultimately forced the Welsh RU to turn a blind eye. Sooner or later, it was inevitable that they would clash head-on with the RFU in England.

Why Does Wales Play The Wrong Type of Rugby?

When the crisis finally erupted, it surrounded a man who had become the symbol of Welsh rugby's rise to glory. Born in 1864, Arthur Gould debuted for Newport as a teenager and led its all-conquering team of the early 1890s before captaining Wales to a Triple Crown in 1893. Such unprecedented success catapulted him thereafter to national celebrity status.

In 1896, on leading Wales to its third victory over England, the *South Wales Argus* and *South Wales Daily News* started a testimonial fund for him. Money poured in. In fact so much was collected that the Welsh RU bought Gould's own house with it and gave it back to him as a gift. The RFU declared this to be a violation of its amateur rules and, in protest, Wales withdrew from union's International Board. It seemed it was now only a matter of time before another 1895-style split.

But then both sides hesitated. The RFU realised that if it expelled Wales it would weaken international rugby union, strengthen the new Northern Union, and deal another blow to its authority. And so, confronted with the stark choice of undermining itself by enforcing amateur rules and expelling Wales, or fudging its amateur principles to maintain unity, the RFU chose the latter.

The RFU's secretary, Rowland Hill, admitted the decision 'was a question of expediency' and issued a statement which declared that although Gould was guilty of professionalism by accepting the gift of his house, 'exceptional circumstances' meant he would not be banned from rugby. F.E. Smith, the future cabinet minister Lord Birkenhead, stated in *The Times* that the decision was made to 'prevent the great accession of strength to the Northern Union which would have followed, had the Welsh Union been driven into their arms.'[2]

The 'Gould compromise' defined the relationship between Welsh rugby and the RFU for the next century. As long as sufficient decorum was maintained, the RFU did not look too closely at Welsh affairs, and ignored covert 'boot money' paid to working-class players. As long as clubs pretended not to pay anyone, the RFU pretended to believe them.

And so the threat of Welsh rugby union breaking from the RFU and joining the Northern Union was averted.

Following which, somewhat ironically, it was the Northern Union that enabled rugby union to become the national sport of Wales. The 1895 split had weakened England so severely that between 1899 and 1909 Wales beat them ten times out of eleven. Even the one they didn't win ended in a draw. Wales's ability to consistently beat England was the crucial factor in making union the Welsh national game – which would not have been possible if English rugby had remained unified.

Ultimately, the leaders of Welsh rugby decided they owed their allegiance to the privately-educated middle classes who ran the RFU, rather than to the miners and steelworkers who were the backbone of the game in South Wales.

The WRU hoped it had locked rugby league out, but could not stop many hundreds of its players going north to openly earn the rewards their talents richly deserved – and grace the sport of rugby league wherever it was staged.

So while Wales itself may have played the wrong type of rugby, those countless Welsh players who went north knew they were playing the right game.

---

[1] *The Yorkshireman*, 3 March 1885.
[2] *The Times*, 18 Oct. 1897.

7.

Why Didn't Lily Parr Play Rugby?

In the 1920s, Lily Parr was the biggest name in women's football. She was the star of the famous Dick, Kerr Ladies FC and, in a career that lasted more than three decades, scored 986 goals for them, more than any other woman footballer has scored in a career before or since.

Lily began playing football with the local St Helens Ladies team in 1919, aged just 14. She was soon poached by Dick, Kerr's, who gave her a job at the engineering factory of the club's owners. She quickly repaid them, scoring 108 goals in her first year. So powerful was she that one of her shots broke the wrist of a male goalkeeper,[1] or so it was claimed by club publicists. She finally retired from football, aged 46, in 1951.

Born in St Helens in 1905, Lily lived little more than a mile from Knowsley Road rugby league ground and, according to her biographers, grew up playing football and rugby with her three brothers. So, if she was raised in a rugby league hotbed and had been taught the game as a girl, why didn't Lily Parr play rugby league?

The short answer is: she never had the opportunity. There were no women's rugby clubs in St Helens – or anywhere else – at that time. So the bigger question is why not?

Women had certainly been fans from the earliest times. When Yorkshire played Lancashire in 1870, in rugby's first Roses Match, journalists reported a 'large number of the fair sex' in the crowd. Nor were women immune from the rugby fever that gripped the north in the 1880s. 'Don't imagine all the spectators were men, for they were not,' noted the weekly *Yorkshireman*'s report on a Yorkshire v Cheshire match in 1883, 'the comments from this portion of the gathering were as numerous and as critical as those of their brothers, husbands and fathers.'[2]

Just like men, going to the rugby gave women chance to escape their traditional roles for a couple of hours each week. In 1884, a woman threw red hot coals at Batley players after they defeated Horbury, while in 1888 Swinton's chairman criticised female fans for their 'bad manners and rowdiness'.[3]

A few miles from Swinton, publican Isabella Boardman was a central figure in the early years of Broughton Rangers, offering her pub as headquarters and changing rooms for the club, while providing material support for Rangers' players. She was so prominent that for years the team was nicknamed 'Mrs Boardman's Boys'. But the rugby authorities drew a line when it came to women as anything other than supporters.

'We have no dealings with women here!' the president of the Yorkshire Rugby Union, the Reverend Frank Marshall, proclaimed in 1889.[4]

The roots of such hostility ran deep. Rugby was developed in the public schools as a way to insulate schoolboys against effeminacy and homosexuality, and turn them into 'real men'.

Why Didn't Lily Parr Play Rugby?

In the eyes of its true believers, rugby was the ultimate man's sport: 'The only game that is absolutely masculine in the country,' according to the president of Salford in 1891,[5] a belief accepted widely. When businessmen organised women's matches between music hall artistes from Scotland in 1881, and in the north of England in 1887, they chose the soccer code. The British Ladies FC, a touring side formed in 1895 that played dozens of exhibition matches, never considered rugby. Even then, opposition to women playing any type of football was so strong that the 1881 and 1887 matches were plagued by hostile and sometimes violent crowd invasions.

So the only chance girls got to play rugby was at home or in the streets with their brothers, as Lily Parr did in the early 1900s. The most famous example was Emily Valentine, ten-year old daughter of a teacher at Enniskillen's Portora Royal School in Northern Ireland, who scored a try in an informal match between male pupils in 1887, often portrayed as the 'William Webb Ellis moment' of women's rugby union.

It would be another three decades before women began playing any football code in significant numbers. World War One brought tens of thousands of women into engineering factories to manufacture guns and shells for the war effort. It was hard and dangerous work and employers tried to raise morale by providing welfare facilities, such as sports halls, playing fields and even time off for players. As soccer was overwhelmingly the most popular sport in Britain, it did not come as a surprise that many women workers chose football.

There was another factor, often overlooked today. World War One was a time of strikes, industrial conflict and the growth of trade unions. Many factories with militant workforces were also pioneers of women's football, which bosses saw as an antidote to female militancy. William Beardmore & Company, a massive engineering works in Glasgow, was one such early promoter in a hotbed of working-class radicalism. In March 1916, future MP David Kirkwood, chief shop steward, was arrested and deported to England after a strike against management's refusal to allow him to speak to women workers. It was also no accident that Vickers' engineering factories in Barrow and Sheffield, both with a reputation for militancy, established well-known women's soccer teams in the aftermath of strikes in 1916 and 1917.

Enthusiasm for women's football boomed between 1917 and 1920. Many factory teams were established in industrial towns and cities with hundreds of matches played to raise money for war charities. Some of the most notable were in Wigan, Leigh, Huddersfield, Whitehaven, St Helens and Barrow, well-known rugby league towns. Yet not a single one of those set up a women's rugby league team.

For many years it was believed that women in the mining village of Featherstone were the first to play organised rugby league in 1921. They aimed to raise money for the families of miners locked-out from work by colliery owners. But recent detailed research from historian Victoria Samantha Dawson has shown this didn't happen. Plans were made for two teams to play but, in May 1921, the *Pontefract and Castleford Express* reported that the women: '...would dearly have liked to play the Northern Union game, about which they know most; but this was scotched by their men-folk, on the grounds that it was too dangerous. So they played Association.'[6]

In short, women who wanted to play rugby league were told it was a man's game, and they should play soccer, a sport viewed in rugby culture as less masculine and more feminine.

This wasn't just the view of rugby league men in Yorkshire. During the miners' lock-out of 1921, women's soccer matches were organised in Wigan. They were nicknamed 'Pea Soup' games because they raised money for soup kitchens to help

Why Didn't Lily Parr Play Rugby?

feed local mining families.[7] But even in Wigan, women's rugby league matches could not take place. Instead, a letter to the *Wigan Examiner* called the round-ball game 'a mollycoddle' and went on to claim 'the Northern Union people can smile when they read about the lady footballers; they can never play rugby. Does this prove which is the man's game?'

It certainly proved that rugby league had missed out on a generation of women players.

The only rugby area which took part in the great wave of women's sport at this time was South Wales. In October 1917, the Newport Box Repairing Factory formed a women's rugby union team to play matches to raise money for war charities. Over the next six months they played nine fixtures, including three against a Cardiff women's side. The third game drew around 10,000 spectators to Cardiff Arms Park. They played at Abergavenny, Abertillery, Barry Island and Cwmbran too, while the Cardiff team also faced Treorchy.

But as with women's soccer, these rugby union teams were short-lived. Once the war ended in November 1918, charity fund raising lost importance, traditional roles of mother and housewife were re-enforced, and women were driven out of factories and back into the home. As Cardiff full-back Maria Eley recalled: 'We loved it. It was such fun with us all playing together on the pitch, but we had to stop when the men came back ... which was a shame. Such great fun we had.'[8]

The only place women did play rugby league during these tumultuous times was 14,000 miles away, in Sydney.

In September 1921, the Metropolitan Blues and Sydney Reds played before a 20,000 crowd at Sydney's Agricultural Showgrounds. Fifteen-year-old Maggie Moloney stole the show by scoring four tries for the victorious Blues. The result was reversed in the return match a week later. The following year the teams played three more matches before disbanding due to lack of support from the rugby league authorities. In 1921, two women's teams were formed in New Zealand, one in the Auckland suburb of Parnell and the other in Hornby, near Christchurch, but they withered on the vine due to the indifference of rugby league officials.[9]

It wasn't until 1953 that the first organised women's rugby league matches in Britain took place. Marsh Blondes and Quay Brunettes met twice in the Marsh and Quay district of Workington. They then combined to play another local team, Dearham Amazons, in front of 2,000 people. Organised to raise money for charities during the royal coronation, the matches were treated seriously by players, spectators and (most of) the press. The potential was there for all to see.

It had, in fact, been there all the time. If rugby league had not been so trapped for so long by masculine pride and fear of effeminacy, the game could have been the sport of choice for women in the industrial towns of the north of England.

And Lily Parr would quite likely be celebrated as a pioneer of women's rugby league in her hometown of St Helens.

---

[1] *Lancashire Daily Post*, 31 Oct 1931.
[2] *The Yorkshireman*, 3 March 1883.
[3] *Salford Reporter*, 2 June 1888.
[4] *The Yorkshireman*, 18 Dec 1889.
[5] *Pendleton Reporter*, 28 Nov 1891.
[6] This and the Wigan quote are from the doctoral thesis of Victoria S. Dawson, *Women and Rugby League: Gender, Class and Community in the North of England, 1880-1970*, (De Montfort University: 2017) pp. 150 and 157.
[7] Alethea Melling, '"Plucky lasses", "pea soup" and politics: the role of ladies' football during the 1921 miners' lock–out in Wigan and Leigh'," *International Journal of the History of Sport*, (1999) 16 (1). pp. 38-64.
[8] The full story of women playing rugby union in World War One can be found in Lydia Furse's PhD thesis *Women in Rugby Union: A Social and Cultural History*, c. 1880-2016 (De Montfort University: 2021). Maria Eley's quote is on p. 117.
[9] Charles Little '"What a freak-show they made!" Women's Rugby League in 1920s Sydney,' *Football Studies* (2001) 4:2, pp. 25-40. Katherine Haines, 'The 1921 Peak and Turning Point in Women's Football History: An Australasian, Cross-Code Perspective,' *International Journal of the History of Sport* (2016) 33:8. pp.1-19.

8.

The Mystery Of Sherlock Holmes's Missing Three-Quarter

What does the cocaine-addicted, violin-playing, Baker Street-based detective Sherlock Holmes have to do with rugby?

Quite a lot in fact, because his creator, Arthur Conan Doyle, was an enthusiastic sportsman and a very keen rugby fan, having taken up the game at school and university.

One of his less-well known Sherlock Holmes stories is 'The Adventure of the Missing Three-Quarter', which first appeared in a 1904 edition of *The Strand* magazine. It is one of the few examples of an adult-targetted tale featuring rugby published during the first few decades of the game's existence.

Of course, there were lots of children's stories about rugby. Its early popularity owed a huge amount to the success of the Thomas Hughes novel *Tom Brown's School Days*, which, while set in the 1830s, essentially began the school story genre when it came out in 1857. But rugby is rarely seen in other types of literature.

Conan Doyle was educated at the rugby stronghold of Stoneyhurst College, a Catholic private school in Lancashire that modelled itself on Rugby School, and he played virtually every type of sport at some point.

Nor was he the only best-selling author in Victorian times who was a rugby fan. Bram Stoker, creator of *Dracula*, was such a good forward as a student at Trinity College, Dublin, that he is mentioned Frank Marshall's 1892 book *Football: The Rugby Union Game*.

For Conan Doyle, rugby was 'the best collective sport. Strength, courage, speed and resource are great qualities to include in a single game,' and he wanted to see it played in all schools. So it's unsurprising, perhaps, that rugby would end up being central to one of his many short stories.

Indeed, Sherlock Holmes himself could be seen as the epitome of rugby union's ideal of the gentleman amateur, solving crimes for pure enjoyment rather than for monetary gain.

'The Adventure of the Missing Three-Quarter' concerns the mysterious disappearance of England player Godfrey Staunton, hours before he was due to represent Cambridge University against Oxford in the Varsity match, then rugby union's most important club match of the season.

Holmes is engaged by Cambridge captain Cyril Overton, who explains that Staunton is one of the best players in the country. The master detective knows nothing of sport but the rugby-loving Dr Watson (who in many ways is based on Conan Doyle himself) is suitably impressed.

It's a rather weak plot which concludes disappointingly by revealing the missing Staunton has simply gone to care for his secret wife, dying of tuberculosis. It's more interesting from a rugby perspective than it is as a mystery. The early pages of the story discuss what makes a good rugby player

The Mystery of Sherlock Holmes's Missing Three-Quarter

and stress the importance of the amateur spirit. Dr Watson explains what makes Staunton so good. Such a three-quarter, he says, not only has to be an expert at passing the ball and tackling, but must be a good dribbler, punter and drop-kicker. This has led to debate among fans of the Holmes stories – known as 'Sherlockians' – who suggest Conan Doyle may have made a mistake in his description of the essential skills of a three-quarter. Even in rugby union, there seems to be no need for a centre or winger to be an expert kicker, let alone a dribbler of the ball. But Conan Doyle knew his stuff.

In the 1890s, when the story is set, union was focused on kicking skills. A penalty goal brought three points, same as a try, and a drop was worth four. Many believed goals were more important than tries, in contrast to northern clubs where it was believed that try-scoring was the 'acme of good play'. Inadvertently then, 'The Adventure of the Missing Three-Quarter' highlights one of the dividing lines over which rugby split in 1895, although as far as we know Conan Doyle never commented on that rupture or the Northern Union.

However, that is most definitely not true of his great friend, Bertram Fletcher Robinson. Born in 1870, Robinson was a well-known journalist and provided some of the inspiration for perhaps the most famous of all Sherlock Holmes stories, 'The Hound of the Baskervilles'.

Like Conan Doyle, Robinson was a keen rugby player, good enough to play for Cambridge in three Varsity matches against Oxford, as well as against Lancashire twice. He was also a committed and vocal supporter of the RFU in its battle against the northern clubs. In 1896, he wrote a book called *Rugby Football*, which describes his experiences in the game, including playing against northern clubs, and condemns the recent formation of the Northern Union.

As well as opposing payments to players, Robinson also

highlighted the different conceptions of the RFU and the Northern Union about how rugby should be played:

> It has been seriously proposed by the Northern Union to alter the rules, and reduce the number of players, in order that the game may be faster and more 'pleasing to the spectators'. I shrewdly suspect that, if the truth be told, they hope, by knocking off two forwards, to be able to save on weekly wages ... A travelling circus of fifteen men is an expensive establishment to keep up.[1]

Not surprisingly given his sarcastic tone, Robinson also became one of the first of many people to predict the death of the NU, barely twelve months after it had been formed. The professional player, he believed, would eventually die out because they would corrupt the sport and, consequently, in the north 'rugby football will disappear with him'.

It didn't.

However, Conan Doyle's books and Robinson's journalism do illustrate how the 1895 rugby split was not just an internal dispute between rugby clubs. They also reflected the state of British society and the concerns of the late Victorian era.

We shouldn't be surprised at this. Rugby is always as much about society as it is about what happens on the field. As Holmes might have put it, this is an elementary fact not just about rugby, but also sport as whole.

---

[1] B.F. Robinson, *Rugby Football* (London: 1896) p. 55.

9.

Unintended Consequences: How The All Blacks Kick-Started Rugby League Down Under

The New Zealand All Blacks' tour of 1905 sparked a rugby revolution. They were the first All Blacks to tour the northern hemisphere and returned home from Britain having won 34 of their 35 matches. The game would never be the same.

No official national rugby team had previously toured the British Isles, although it wasn't for want of trying. The idea emerged with the formation of the New Zealand RU in 1892, but it wasn't until 1903 that the RFU agreed to host the Kiwis.

In 1888, the predominantly Maori, and unofficial, Native New Zealand tourists had left a bitter taste in RFU mouths. Not only had they been widely suspected of professionalism, but they had openly accused the England team of cheating. The fact that a predominately non-white team defeated many British teams also seemed to threaten the social and racial hierarchy beloved of the RFU leaders. It took almost two decades for the wounds to heal.

The scene was set for the 1905 tour by the visit to New Zealand of David Bedell-Sivright's 1904 British tourists. The first two matches were won narrowly by the Brits, though not without controversy. The British objected to New Zealand's scrummaging tactics, which used a seven-forward formation of two front-row forwards to hook the ball out of the scrum, three second-rowers and two back-rowers, plus a 'wing-forward' who would feed the ball in and then shield the scrum-half at its back once the ball came out.

For their part, the New Zealanders were shocked at the physicality of their opponents. The play of captain Bedell-Sivright, about whom it was said 'his conception of football was one of trained violence', caused much antagonism, as did the widespread belief that the British side quickly resorted to gamesmanship when it suited them.[1]

The final and decisive Test match was won 9-3 by the New Zealanders, with winger (and future rugby league pioneer) Duncan MacGregor crossing for two tries. 'Every young New Zealander today will feel an inch taller because of the victory that was won at Wellington by the football champions of the colony,' said the *New Zealand Herald*. Anticipation for the following year's tour of Britain could not have been higher.

Nevertheless, when the All Blacks did finally dock at Plymouth on 8 September 1905 no-one in Britain or New Zealand had the slightest inkling of the tsunami to come.

It began in Newton Abbot eight days later. Within three minutes of the opening match against Devon, the All Black five-eighth Jimmy Hunter ran in for the opening try of the tour. Seventy-seven minutes later, the All Blacks had scored a further 11 tries to win by an amazing 55-4. Their opponents, who would be crowned English county champions the following year, could only manage a single drop-goal in the final minutes.

How The All Blacks Kick-Started RL Down Under

To show it was no fluke, the All Blacks then scored another 11 tries in a 41-0 rout of Cornwall. It wasn't until their seventh match, against the reigning county champions Durham, that the All Blacks' defence finally gave up a try. But their tries kept on coming. The All Blacks were not only fitter but vastly more skilled and tactically sophisticated than the English. Crucially, they also approached the game with a different attitude. Their focus was on running, passing and scoring tries. Unbelievably for a rugby union team, they scored more than twice as many tries as goals: 205 to 102.

Nowhere was this difference more apparent than in their attitude to penalties. Instead of going for goal when awarded one, the New Zealanders invariably ran the ball. They kicked only four penalty goals on the entire tour. As rugby lovers in the north of England noted, the All Blacks played like a professional Northern Union team.

In the Test matches, neither Ireland nor England came anywhere near the Kiwis. Both lost 15-0, England conceding five tries on a quagmire of a pitch, four going to Duncan MacGregor. Scotland led at half-time, but lost 12-7.

How could there be such a gap between the 'Mother Country' of the British Empire and a colony whose population numbered fewer than a million? Some journalists argued that physical 'degeneracy' was the result of an industrial, urban lifestyle undermining the fitness of the population. But the simple fact was that English rugby was divided in two. Moreover, soccer claimed a majority of Britain's best athletes. In New Zealand rugby union had no winter competitor for sporting talent.

This could be seen in December 1905 when the All Blacks moved to Wales, a nation where union ruled supreme. Club sides Newport, Cardiff and Swansea all tested the All Blacks to the limit, losing by three, two and one-point margins.

The biggest test came against Wales itself in December. Aware this would be rugby's version of a world heavyweight boxing title fight, the Welsh had been preparing for it almost since the New Zealanders arrived. They sought to nullify the All Blacks by keeping it tight and dominating their forwards.

Full-back Bert Winfield's kicking constantly pinned the All Blacks in their own half, restricting their ability to run the ball. Stealing a leaf from the tourists' book, Newport's Cliff Pritchard was used as a wing-forward, allowing the Welsh to diminish the impact of New Zealand captain and wing-forward, Dave Gallaher.

To counter New Zealand's 2-3-2 formation in the scrum, the wily Welsh waited for their opponents to pack down and then used their three-man front row to seize the loose head. This deprived the All Blacks of so much possession that some journalists wondered if they'd stopped contesting for the ball.

When winger Teddy Morgan scored Wales' try on the half-hour, it seemed the tide had turned. But when Bob Deans cut through the Welsh defence to seemingly score late in the second half, Welsh hopes seemed to have been dashed.

However, Deans' try was disallowed and Wales held on to a victory that cemented union as its national passion. But for the New Zealanders, the disallowed try was the grit in the oyster of the greatest tour, a grievance the All Blacks would forever seek to avenge.

Yet this Welsh victory could not fundamentally change the volcanic impact the 1905 All Black tour had. As soon as they arrived home in 1906, New Zealand's players discovered that they would not benefit from a hugely profitable venture. Discontent soon turned to open rebellion and dissatisfaction.

Barely a year later, four of the original All Blacks provided the backbone of the first-ever New Zealand rugby league team to tour Britain in 1907. And the rugby rebellion did not

How The All Blacks Kick-Started RL Down Under

stop there, as the 'professional All Blacks' (as league's tourists were officially named) became the lightning rod for a players' revolt in Australian rugby union, which led to the formation of rugby league in that nation too. Within five years, rugby league had overtaken rugby union in Australia and was well-established in Auckland and other industrial working-class regions in New Zealand.

The All Blacks of 1905 had indeed revolutionised rugby, but not in the way that rugby union's administrators had hoped.

---

[1] Said by Wallaby captain Dr Herbert Moran in *Viewless Winds* (London: 1939) p. 46.

10.

Did Australian Rugby Union Lose The Code War Because It Was Too Patriotic?

If you've ever been involved in a debate between Australian rugby union and league fans, you'll have noticed how, before long, someone will raise the question of what happened in World War One.

League, so the argument goes, only became the dominant code in Australia because union chose to stop playing during the war. Rugby league continued to be played throughout the hostilities and so gained an unfair advantage over the more patriotic rugby union. But as usual in the rugby code wars all is not as straightforward as it may appear. In fact, the dispute reflects a much deeper division in Australian society at the time about support for the conflict.

When Britain declared war on Germany on 4 August 1914, all the nations of the British Empire were automatically at war with Germany too. So without any consultation or debate, Australia also found itself a combatant. Just as on the other

How Australian Rugby Union Lost The Code War

side of the world, the Australian football codes had differing opinions about what they should do. 'The Great War' had begun just as Australia's 1914 rugby season was ending, so attention focused on whether sport should resume in 1915. In Britain, rugby league and soccer decided to continue, as did the Victorian Football League, the premier Australian Rules competition. But, in April 1915, the New South Wales Rugby Union in Sydney decided to suspend all league and representative matches for the duration of the fighting.

Taking their lead from the RFU, rugby union proclaimed itself as the only sport doing its patriotic duty. And it was this assertion which laid the basis for the view that union lost out to league because it was more patriotic.

The reality was not so simple. Although the New South Wales RU was the governing body of Australian union in all but name, it was only in Sydney that competitive rugby was fully suspended. Union tournaments continued to be played throughout 1915 in most of the rest of New South Wales and Queensland. For example, Christian Brothers 'A' team won the Queensland premiership in September 1915 while, in NSW, the Hunter Rugby Union Championship final was drawn 0-0 between West End and Newcastle.

But even in Sydney itself, friendlies continued to be played throughout 1915. For example in June of that year, Norths, Easts, Mosman, St George, Sydney University, Manly, Randwick and South Sydney union sides all staged matches. Towards the end of the season, knock-out competitions were also played. Far from there being no rugby union, the game continued but on a less structured and less competitive basis.

It was only in 1916 that the Queensland RU finally decided to suspend fixtures in Brisbane and even then regional unions continued to organise local competitions. A cursory look at newspapers of the day will show that premierships were still awarded in Central Queensland, the Hunter Valley, Bathurst, and many other places. Even in Sydney, the lower-grade Metropolitan Cup competition was played.

The 1917 season saw regular matches played in Sydney between leading club sides, some of whom had merged for the duration of the war. On 8 September that year, *The Arrow*, a Sydney sports weekly, adorned its front page with a photograph of the temporarily-merged Glebe-Balmain rugby union club, describing how the team had just gone through the 1917 season with only two defeats.

So, contrary to the commonly-accepted story, Australian rugby union did not stop playing the game during World War One. As was often the case, most obviously with regard to amateur regulations, union had made its own decision and then claimed the moral high ground from which it criticised those who disagreed with it. The dispute with rugby league about World War One was one more example of this.

In fact, the decision of the New South Wales Rugby Union to allow its clubs to continue playing any matches during the war would have been seen as unpatriotic by the Rugby Football Union in England. The RFU forbade all club matches whatsoever from being played for the duration of the war, and was at the forefront of criticising the Football League for continuing to play soccer, whether competitive or friendly. Its supporters viewed soccer and rugby league as being disloyal for allowing clubs to play football in war-time.

Despite this criticism, the leadership of Australian rugby league saw itself no less patriotic than rugby union. The New South Wales Rugby League encouraged its players to enlist and argued that its competitions helped to promote civilian morale during war-time – as would rugby union itself during World War Two, when it continued to play competitive rugby throughout that conflict.

How Australian Rugby Union Lost The Code War

The first prominent Australian player of either code to be killed in action was Ted Larkin, first full-time secretary of the New South Wales Rugby League, who died at Gallipoli on 4 May 1915. Many more players of both codes would also have their lives cut needlessly short by the global barbarism.

And the rugby codes were not the only ones to split over it. In Melbourne, Australian Rules football was wracked by conflict over Britain's declaration of war. In Victoria, the president of the Metropolitan Amateur Football Association (MAFA), Lawrence Adamson, sarcastically declared in 1914 that those professional players of the Victorian Football League (today's AFL) who continued to play during the war ought to be given the German Iron Cross, instead of a premiership medal, for their services to the Kaiser.

In 1915, the VFL's rival league, the Victorian Football Association, voted to stop playing for the duration. The VFL itself was split down the middle about what to do. It voted narrowly to stop playing in 1915, but the season continued because its constitution required a majority of three-quarters for binding decisions. In 1916, only four of the ten pre-war VFL clubs took the field, a number that grew to six in 1917.

Such divisions reveal a nation deeply divided.

Although Britain's declaration of war was wholeheartedly supported by Australia's middle and upper classes, it was not so popular among many in the working class. In particular, millions of Australians of Irish heritage were not keen to support a country that denied the national rights of Ireland.

In Brisbane, the driving force behind the establishment of rugby league was leading Labour politician Jack Fihelly, also one of the managers of the first Kangaroo tour to Britain. He became the focus of opposition to militarism, so much so the term 'Fihelly-ism' was coined to describe the hostility of Irish-Australians to the war.

Opposition was not confined to those with links to Ireland however. In October 1916, the Australian government held a referendum to win support for compulsory conscription into the army. A narrow majority voted against. In December 1917, another referendum was held, resulting in an even larger anti-conscription majority. Between the two ballots, NSW and Victoria were wracked by a partial general strike in August 1917, when tens of thousands of workers downed tools in defence of their rights. Once again, sporting divisions merely reflected those in society at large.

In reality, the war had little bearing on rugby union's fall from grace or rugby league's rise to become the dominant code. League had won that battle long before World War One.

By 1910, just a couple of years after Australian rugby had split, league crowds dwarfed union's. Tom Hickie, Australia's leading historian of rugby union, has argued that the game's policy towards the war simply exacerbated its fundamental difficulties: 'League had won the support of Sydney's football public before 1914, [and] the decision by the NSWRU to suspend competition during the years 1915-18 only widened the gap in the levels of support.'[1]

Once again, like amateurism or the loss of players to the thirteen-a-side game, the problems faced by rugby union during and after the First World War were not caused by rugby league. They were a self-inflicted wound.

---

[1] Thomas V. Hickie, *A Sense of Union* (Sydney 1998) p. 97.

11.

Why The 'First Lions' Weren't The First (And Weren't Even Lions)

Flick through any recent book on the history of British rugby union and you will read that the very first Lions tour was to Australia and New Zealand in 1888. Look at the Lions' official website and it's the same story.

But it *wasn't* a Lions tour.

It is true the first-ever British rugby tour down under took place in 1888, but the side was not called the Lions. They were unofficial tourists, covertly semi-professional and most definitely not recognised by the RFU or the game's newly formed International Rugby Board.

In contemporary newspapers and the classic 1892 history of rugby, *Football: The Rugby Union Game*, the side in question was known as 'Shaw and Shrewsbury's Australian Team', after the two businessmen who organised the trip. The first British Isles rugby union outfit to be called the Lions was the 1950 squad that went to New Zealand, sixty-two years later.

In contrast, The British rugby league team had been known as the Lions ever since its first tour down under in 1910.

The RFU did everything it could to discourage players from joining the 1888 tour down under, including banning one of its stars, Jack Clowes, for a £15 expenses payment.

The Australians had invited the RFU to take a team out to the Southern Hemisphere in the late 1870s, but the English leaders of the sport showed little interest beyond the British Isles. However, the huge popularity of rugby across Britain, Australia and New Zealand in the 1880s raised the interest of entrepreneurs, especially those in professional cricket.

Cricket's first official England tour to Australia had taken place in 1876, so lucrative teams that went almost every year thereafter. So it was no surprise when two veteran organisers, Nottinghamshire's Alfred Shaw and Arthur Shrewsbury, announced a rugby tour to Australia and New Zealand in 1888. It was a purely commercial venture, as Shaw conceded openly: 'We arranged the trip in the hope of making money'.

RFU secretary Rowland Hill refused either to 'support or approve' it and warned players if they accepted anything more than strict travel expenses they would be banned for violating amateur regulations. For men such as Shaw and Shrewsbury, RFU amateurism suited their purposes perfectly, as Shrewsbury admitted shortly before departure: 'If the rugby union can get players to come out without [us paying them] all the better for us.'[1]

Captained by Swinton forward Bob Seddon, 14 of the 22 selected were from clubs that would create the Northern Union a few years later. Three came from the small industrial town of Hawick in the Scottish Borders, and one each from Edinburgh and Cambridge universities. An unattached 'gentleman' also joined the party and one came from Douglas on the Isle of Man. Also on board was Andrew Stoddart, the

Why The 'First Lions' Weren't The First

future England cricket and rugby captain, who also played rugby for Blackheath.

Ahead of the trip, Halifax's Jack Clowes was called before the RFU committee and cross-examined about the £15 expenses given to him by Shaw and Shrewsbury. By the time the RFU reached a decision and declared him a professional, the party had already set sail, placing him in the unfortunate position of being banned from playing rugby while on tour.

Clowes was not the only one paid. Stoddart was given a down payment of £50 beforehand. How much he eventually received is unclear, but we do know that two lesser-known amateurs were offered £200 'expenses' to make the trip. WH Thomas of Cambridge University and Wales was paid £90 for his thirty weeks on tour and tried to negotiate a further £3 per week when it was unexpectedly lengthened. As well as this, touring as a gentleman amateur had other advantages, as can be seen in Shrewsbury asking Shaw to specify which 'amateurs you have promised to pay their wine and refreshment account at dinners.'

The tourists arrived in New Zealand for the first leg on 23 April. Over the next month they won six out of nine, drawing with Wellington, losing to powerful Auckland and Taranaki. The New Zealanders were taken aback by how they heeled the ball out of scrums and the speed with which they passed the ball among the backs. These were lessons they would take to heart, eventually the hallmarks of New Zealand rugby.

The British side then went back across the Tasman Sea to Sydney for the first half of the Australian leg, winning four matches and drawing one. They then went to the Melbourne suburb of Carlton to play their first-ever game of Victorian Rules football. It was not a success. Carlton FC – one of the biggest names in the Victorian game – ran amok, scoring fourteen goals to the tourists' three.

As would be expected from a team of talented athletes, the more the tourists played Victorian Rules the better they got. Eventually they managed to win seven of nineteen matches in the unfamiliar code, but overall it was not a pleasant experience. They were glad to get back to rugby: 'I imagine that none of our men like the Victorian game,' captain Bob Seddon told Sydney's weekly *The Referee*.[2]

'Shaw and Shrewsbury's Australian Team' then went through New South Wales, Queensland and a second leg in New Zealand without losing. In November, they left for Britain having won twenty-seven of their thirty-five games.

The 1888 British tour once and for all established that rugby would be the game of NSW and Queensland. They attracted the biggest crowds ever seen there. And the sport became a tangible link with the place that even those born and raised in Australia called 'Home'.

It also had a deeper cultural impact. As the Australian press noted, the majority of the tourists were men from the industrial working classes in the north of England. Rugby in Sydney and Brisbane was traditionally the preserve of the upper and middle classes, but the tourists demonstrated that it was equally a game for those who earned a living through manual labour. To compete successfully against overseas visitors, wrote *The Referee*, 'I should like to see ... the working-man element introduced into our clubs.'[3]

When the tourists arrived home, journalists expected the RFU to ban them on the grounds of professionalism. Yet to everyone's surprise, the RFU lifted its ban on Jack Clowes and the matter was quietly dropped.

The reason was simple: any investigation into the finances of the tourists would have implicated Andrew Stoddart and the other gentlemen on the trip – the RFU would have had to ban one of England's leading sportsmen. By ignoring both its

Why The 'First Lions' Weren't The First

own regulations and overwhelming evidence of payments, the RFU laid bare the underlying class bias of the amateur ethos: a middle class gentleman was by definition amateur, whether paid or not, and not to be judged by the standards of other, working class, fellows.

No wonder that for the best part of a century rugby union ignored the 1888 tourists. But the advent of professionalism in the 1990s and growth of the Lions as a commercial brand have meant that its marketing now reaches further back into history, the better to create a tradition that has the legitimacy of the distant past. Who needs historical accuracy?

The men who led rugby union in its first hundred years would have been horrified. The 1888 tourists represented everything they had rejected: commercialism, professionalism and the dominance of the working class. To them, the tourists had sullied the amateur virtues of rugby.

Scorned by the RFU but welcomed in Australia's industrial centres, meanwhile, those tourists had little in common with subsequent rugby union tours by the British and Irish Lions.

On the other hand, this was a team of predominantly working class northern players who had no qualms about accepting payments for their rugby talents.

Bob Seddon – a warehouseman born in Salford – and teammates paved the way for men such as Harold Wagstaff, Jim Sullivan and Alan Prescott, industrial workers who in later years would also go on to captain Lions tours of Australia and New Zealand. If anyone can claim the legacy of the pioneering 1888 rugby tourists, it's not rugby union's Lions, but Great Britain's Rugby League Lions.

---

[1] Arthur Shrewsbury to Alfred Shaw, 18 January 1888, quoted in my *Rugby's Great Split* (Abingdon, 2006) p. 58, from where the pair's other quotes are taken.
[2] Quoted in Sean Fagan, *The First Lions of Rugby* (Melbourne: 2013) p. 214.
[3] 'Football Notes' in *The Referee* (Sydney) 9 Aug 1888.

12.

Inner City Blues (And Reds): How Manchester Was Lost By Rugby

There is a strong case to see Manchester today as the world capital of football. Yet at the start of the 20th century, it was common to think of the place not as a soccer hotbed, but a stronghold of rugby.

In fact, for most of the 19th century, Manchester was one of the most important cities in rugby, a centre of the movement that gave birth to rugby league, and with a strong claim to be the first major rugby city outside of London.

As in so many places in the north of England, the first type of 'football' played there was rugby, not soccer, its first fixture staged in 1857. In 1860, Manchester FC was founded as a rugby club, and Swinton were formed in 1866.

This was a full generation before today's giants emerged. The forerunner of Manchester United, Newton Heath, was formed in 1878 and Ardwick, City's ancestor, two years later. The same year Ardwick FC was formed, no less an authority

How Manchester Was Lost To Rugby

than *The Times* told its readers: 'In the North, the Leeds, Wakefield and Manchester clubs are prominent among a people who are one and all enthusiasts for the [rugby] game.'[1]

Rugby in Lancashire was controlled by the patrician Manchester FC, supported by the equally elite Liverpool club. Both were comprised of young men who were solicitors, bankers, doctors and heirs to merchants and manufacturers. When the Lancashire Rugby Union was set up in 1881, Manchester FC officials were automatically given the positions of president, vice-president, secretary and treasurer. If this wasn't enough, all of Lancashire's county fixtures were to be played at the club's Whalley Range ground.

But by the mid-1880s the growth of soccer in Lancashire had become a cause for concern for rugby. The Lancashire FA Cup competition started in 1879, followed by a plethora of local soccer competitions. Just as importantly, the success of Blackburn's Olympic and Rovers in winning the FA Cup highlighted the nationwide interest the code could bring. Neighbouring towns soon wanted to emulate this success.

Preston had been a rugby town since the 1870s but, following the example of Preston North End's conversion in 1881, virtually all its clubs had switched to association by 1882. Burnley also began as a rugby club before changing codes in the same era. Chorley FC made the switch in 1883.

Many of the key personalities in Lancashire soccer also began their sporting careers as rugby players. Prominent ex-rugger types included Preston's William Sudell, a key mover in bringing professionalism to soccer, T.Y. Ritson, founder of Bolton and District FA, and future Football League presidents Charles Sutcliffe and John McKenna, along with secretary Tom Charnley.

At the Lancashire RU's 1886 annual general meeting, a number of speakers expressed concern about the burgeoning popularity of soccer and its impact on rugby. Werneth FC, near Oldham, proposed that a Lancashire Cup be started, modelled on the Yorkshire Cup, in order to rekindle interest.

The Werneth delegate said that 'the association game was progressing rapidly and [that] the only way to help the rugby game in Lancashire was by a cup competition.' However the county authorities opposed introducing a Lancashire Cup to popularise the sport, and rugby's 'first mover advantage' continued to slip away.

In 1892, Salford official A.A. Sutherland, also the football correspondent of the socialist *Clarion* newspaper, put the blame for soccer's rise firmly on the rugby union authorities:

> Less than ten years ago not a single association club could be found either in Manchester or district. Now both Newton Heath and Ardwick are high up and making big names for themselves at the dribbling code, and have innumerable imitators in their districts. To go further afield, Preston, Southport, Bolton, Bury, Chorley, Little Lever, Bootle, Walton and other clubs which stood high up in Rugby circles have all been absorbed by the associationists ... those who profess to look after the best interests of [rugby] are content to sit still whilst the tide of association football makes great inroads into the stronghold of the rugby game. It is apparent to the ordinary observer that unless some reform is instituted, rugby football in Lancashire is in danger of being swamped.[2]

In those Lancashire towns where rugby had local cup competitions, it could keep ahead. The West Lancashire and Border Towns Cup was started in 1886 and consistently attracted five-figure crowds matches featuring Wigan, St Helens, Warrington and Widnes and eight other sides.

At a town level, eighteen thousand people watched the final of the Wigan Challenge Cup in 1886. Sixteen sides

How Manchester Was Lost To Rugby

contested the first Rochdale Charity Cup in 1887 and thirteen sides took part in the Warrington junior cup competition in 1888, the same year 10,000 people watched that year's final of the Rochdale Cup. But the union authorities undermined even these efforts to popularise the game. The South East Lancashire Cup began in 1884, with clubs based around Manchester, but was shut down in 1889 after the Lancashire Rugby Union investigated it for professionalism.

Some rugby areas decided things were so bad they were prepared to defy rugby's leadership and start their own leagues, viewed by the RFU and its supporters as almost as bad as professionalism itself. By 1892, the Manchester and District, North West, South East Lancashire and West Lancashire leagues were all in existence.

In June of 1892, Swinton called a meeting in Manchester to discuss the formation of a Lancashire-wide county league of leading teams. They were supported by Salford, Broughton Rangers, Oldham, Warrington and Wigan. Trying to keep control of a volatile situation, the Lancashire Rugby Union accepted their demands in September 1892 and voted to start a Lancashire club championship.

But the new league came too late to counteract the appeal of the FA Cup and the Football League in Lancashire, whose clubs had won the FA cup eight times in the previous decade, along with three of the first four Football League titles. Soccer had become so powerful that, in 1893, the Manchester FA asked for its own seat on the FA council because of its success in popularising soccer in 'the stronghold of Rugbyism'.

In that same year over 45,000 people watched the FA Cup final at Manchester's Fallowfield stadium, setting a record attendance. This massive crowd shocked rugby supporters and delighted soccer followers. By this time, soccer leagues had also been established in most traditional rugby towns.

Professional soccer clubs would soon be formed in Oldham, Rochdale and Wigan.

Loss of players and spectators even affected the gentlemen amateurs of Manchester FC. Lancashire's leading rugby club voted to wind itself up in March 1895 after it was revealed it had accrued liabilities of £409, although this decision was later rescinded.

The formation of the Northern Union breathed life back into Lancashire rugby. However, only Broughton Rangers joined the rebellion in 1895. Salford and Swinton stayed loyal to the RFU initially, but within months realised their mistake as crowds fell through the floor and union clubs in the south refused to travel north to play them.

In April 1896, Salford held a special general meeting to discuss the NU. Committeeman Mr Daniels proposed joining it, pointing out: '[As] Salford was a working class club and didn't contain any so-called gentlemen it would be very nice for the players to have a present of six shillings worth of silver every week. If they continued on amateur lines they would go to smash. They all knew that working class clubs were better supported than clubs such as Liverpool or Manchester.' Of the 400 people at the meeting, only three opposed.

Swinton's switch to the Northern Union received similar overwhelming support at their 1896 general meeting, at which it was pointed out that income had slumped from £1,016 to £383 and season ticket holders had halved over the past four years. Vindication of their decision was quick in coming: in their first two seasons in the NU they made record profits of £450 and £529.

For a short period, the Manchester region recaptured some of its former glory. Broughton Rangers were the outstanding Lancashire club of the early years of rugby league. In 1902, they became the first to do the double, cantering away with

How Manchester Was Lost To Rugby

the Championship and defeating Salford 15-6 to win the Challenge Cup. Salford also finished second and Swinton fourth in the league.

But rugby could never close the gap soccer had established in the 1880s and 1890s. Following World War One, Broughton Rangers struggled from crisis to crisis and eventually went out of the league in 1955. In a telling piece of irony, their former home ground at The Cliff was bought by Manchester United and remained United's training ground until 1999.

The seeds sown by soccer in the 1880s grew into trees whose branches almost strangled rugby. If Lancashire rugby's leaders had taken different decisions in the Victorian era, perhaps Salford, Swinton and Broughton Rangers would be global brands today, and Ardwick and Newton Heath would be nestled in their shadows.

---

[1] *The Times*, 12 Nov 1880.
[2] *Clarion*, 2 April 1892.

13.

The Pen Is Mightier Than The Ball? How *Tom Brown's School Days* Launched Rugby

In 2007, Melvyn Bragg produced a BBC radio series: *12 Books That Changed The World*. Along with the Bible and Charles Darwin's *Origin of the Species*, he included the Football Association's 1863 rules of football.

Leaving aside the fact the 1863 rules bear little resemblance to football's later rules that swept across the globe, the reality is rules did little to spread the popularity of football of any code. It's a bit like describing the popularity of the Beatles by looking at their sheet music.

However, there was one book that did more to popularise all forms of the game – *Tom Brown's School Days*. Written by Thomas Hughes and published by Macmillan in April 1857, it was a runaway best seller, creating the first schoolboy hero.

Based on Hughes's own experience at Rugby School, the novel tells the story of young Tom Brown, son of a country squire, there. Through a series of moral lessons, some learnt

The Pen Is Mightier Than The Ball?

from football and cricket, he matures into a model Victorian gentleman. In a rather heavy-handed way, Tom learns the principles of what was termed Muscular Christianity: team work, fair play, moral certainty and British nationalism. If you've read *Harry Potter*, substitute Quidditch for rugby and wizardry for Christianity; you've pretty much got the picture.

As soon as he arrives, Tom is thrust into a ferocious rugby match. Showing bravery and a sense of duty, in the final minute he dives on a loose ball to save a certain try and wins the match for his team. For most readers, this was a thrilling introduction to the Rugby School version of football, and it inspired countless people to want to play it. Shortly after they were formed in 1864 the first adult rugby team in Leeds wrote to Rugby School asking for a match, so impressed were they by the description. Rugby football also became the sport of choice of the numerous private schools that sprang up in the Victorian era, for whom *Tom Brown's School Days* doubled as an educational guidebook.

It sold eleven thousand copies in its first year and was reprinted almost fifty times by the end of the century. In 1891, Pitman & Sons even published an edition written in shorthand. *The Times'* reviewer called it a book 'every English father might well wish to see in the hands of his son'.[1] It made football morally respectable, fashionable and aspirational.

Football at Rugby was more than sport. It symbolised the school's unique style of education. Unlike its more socially-elite rivals like Eton and Harrow, Rugby placed its emphasis on developing a boy's character, enabling him to become a leader of British society, industry and empire. Competitive sport was a training ground for the struggle for new markets and colonies, an education in the spirit of capitalism, which drove imperial expansion. And Rugby football especially so.

The real hero of *Tom Brown's School Days*, though, was not

Tom Brown. It was Rugby's headmaster, Thomas Arnold, whose presence towers over it. Appointed in 1828, Arnold moved away from a traditional public school curriculum of Latin and Greek towards modern subjects like mathematics, science and languages. *Tom Brown's School Days* depicted the overwhelming sense of moral certainty. Its pupils came to see themselves, in the words of *The Times* reviewer, 'as members of a semi-political, semi-sacerdotal society; [with] an inclination to extend the monitorial system to the world' – a comment similar to many made about rugby union itself over the years.

This moral framework was unremittingly masculine – indeed, one central message was the danger of effeminacy. 'Don't you ever talk about home, or your mother and sisters,' Tom says to a boy at one point. The book also remarks how a new boy might be 'called Molly, or Jenny, or some derogatory feminine name.'[2] There was no room for women or girls.

More shockingly, especially in a book seen as opposing bullying, an effeminate boy is portrayed as a legitimate target. At one point Tom and his best friend East are approached by 'one of the miserable little pretty white-handed curly-headed boys, petted and pampered by some of the big fellows, who wrote their verses for them, taught them to drink and use bad language, and did all they could to spoil them for everything in this world and the next.'[3]

The boy asks for help but without provocation they trip and kick him. As they leave, Tom says: 'Thank goodness, no big fellow ever took to petting me,' to which East replies 'You'd never have been like that.' In a footnote Hughes said 'many boys will know why [this passage] is left in.'[4] Shockingly, the book implies that bullying is acceptable when directed against a boy who is believed to be homosexual.

The huge sales of *Tom Brown's School Days* brought football and its Muscular Christian principles to a new and wider

The Pen Is Mightier Than The Ball?

audience – and not just in Britain, but across the English-speaking world.

In the Empire's white settler colonies – Australia, Canada, New Zealand and South Africa – it quickly acquired the status of a cultural bible. Despite living thousands of miles from what they referred to as the 'Mother Country', colonists were proudly British and rushed to embrace the message of the book, making it a best-seller across the empire. As soon as copies arrived from London, the *Sydney Morning Herald* hailed the book as 'so hearty, its good sense so strong and so thoroughly national, its morality so high, and yet so simple and practical ... we venture to prophesy for it an extended and permanent popularity.'[5]

In the southern state of Victoria – until 1901, Australia was a collection of individual colonies rather than a single nation – Melbourne's *Argus* newspaper chided readers who did not understand the value of football: 'Let those who fancy there is little in the game read the account of one of the Rugby matches ... detailed in that most readable work, *Tom Brown's School Days*, and they will speedily alter their opinion.'[6]

In South Africa in 1862 the first recorded games of football took place in Port Elizabeth and Cape Town. The Cape Town match took place between a Civil Service side and a Military team of officers drawn largely from the 11th Regiment based there. The local press was quick to link the game to the book: the match displayed 'strength and science worthy of *Tom Brown's School Days*', wrote the *Cape Argus*.[7]

In the United States, *Tom Brown* sold 225,000 copies in its first year, a model for educationalists and sportsmen alike. Americans also began to see sport as an important way of passing on moral values to boys and young men. In 1872 the *New York World* daily newspaper even reproduced the book's opening description of a game of rugby as part of its coverage of the inaugural Yale-Columbia football match. Walter Camp, the so-called 'father of American football' was a fan and Teddy Roosevelt, US president from 1901 to 1909, famously said *Tom Brown* was one of two books everyone should read. It is not unconnected that football played with an oval ball became the premier code in these English-speaking countries.

Outside the English-speaking world, the book's biggest influence was in France. As a teenager, Pierre de Coubertin, remembered today as the founder of the modern Olympics, was one of legions of readers who had been captivated by it. He came to idolise Thomas Arnold and made his first visit to Rugby school in 1883. The book's principles became the founding principles of French rugby union. Coubertin even refereed French rugby's first championship final. Perhaps more significantly, it also provided the basis for the Olympics that, today, continue its self-satisfied world of moral certainty.

And that is why *Tom Brown's School Days* – and not the original FA rulebook – is the book that shaped the modern sporting world. Within its pages, rugby for the first time had an importance above and beyond the intrinsic enjoyment of chasing a ball around a field.

Henceforth, it was no longer just a game. For the apostles of Tom Brown, rugby football was a guide to life.

---

[1] *The Times*, 9 Oct 1857.
[2] Thomas Hughes, *Tom Brown's School Days* (Oxford World Classics edition: 1989) pp. 223 & 218.
[3] *Tom Brown's School Days*, pp. 233-4.
[4] *Tom Brown's School Days*, p. 235 & 233.
[5] *Sydney Morning Herald*, 16 Oct 1857.
[6] The Argus, 16 Aug 1858.
[7] *Cape Argus*, 8 Sept 1862, quoted in Jonty Winch, 'Unlocking the Cape Code: Establishing British Football in South Africa', *Sport in History* (2010) 30:4. p. 503.

14.

Rugby's Line-Out And Soccer's Throw-In: Separated At Birth?

There are seven types of modern football – soccer, rugby league, rugby union, American football, Australian Rules, Canadian football and Gaelic football – and they all share one major issue: what to do when the ball goes out of play?

Folk football games of pre-industrial times were played across fields and through villages, where there were no artificial boundaries and play simply went wherever the ball did. But the modern codes have a strictly defined playing area and, when the ball goes over the sideline, the match has to stop and there has to be a way to bring it back into play.

In the mid-1800s, the football codes were essentially one sport with minor rule variations, so it is not surprising that each came up with the same solution – throw it back.

Sheffield Football Club's first rules of 1859 specified that the first player to touch the ball down when it went over the sideline 'must bring it to the edge of touch, and throw it straight out at least six yards from touch.' When the original rules of the Football Association were agreed in 1863, rule five stated: 'When the ball is in touch the first player who touches it shall throw it from the point on the boundary line where it left the ground, in a direction at right angles with the boundary line.'

This is why said 'boundary line' became known as the 'touch line', due to the first rules specifyng that the ball must be touched down before it could be returned to play.

And to emphasise the similarity of the early football codes, both the Football Association and Aussie Rules shared with rugby the rule that the ball could not be thrown backwards or forwards, but only thrown back into play at right angles.

It wasn't until 1877 that the Football Association allowed a throw in any direction. In his excellent book, *The Football Association 1863-1883: A Source Book,* Tony Brown says that the Sheffield Association originally proposed to the FA that the throw-in should be replaced by a kick-in, something that would actually be introduced into rugby league in 1897.

In rugby union, things were slightly more complicated. The first rules of the Rugby Football Union of 1871 gave three options when the ball went into touch. The first was a throw-in at right angles to the touch line, as was then the case in soccer and remains the rugby union rule today.

The second option allowed a player to bring the ball back into play by putting it down on the pitch no more than fifteen yards from the spot it went into touch. When the ball was on the ground, a scrum would be formed around it. Choosing a line-out or a scrum when the ball was kicked into touch was only abolished in Britain in 1939 and worldwide in 1946.

The third option allowed the player to bounce it out from touch and then carry or kick it themselves. This option died out quite quickly as opponents would gather near the point where the ball went in touch to stop the ball carrier bouncing

Line-Outs and Throw-Ins: Separated At Birth?

it to themselves, but it wasn't removed from the RFU rule book until 1911.

As rugby exploded in popularity in the 1880s, the pressure to win intensified, and clubs found that the line-out was easy to disrupt. Lifting was strictly forbidden, but foul play and spoiling tactics were endless. In the north of England, where players and crowds wanted to see open running rugby, calls began to be heard for reform or even abolition of the line-out, not least because it inevitably led to a scrum.

As the dispute over payments to players gathered pace before the 1895 split, so too did the debate on rules. Even this was not free of class prejudice. Dual-rugby and cricket international Frank Mitchell argued that the line-out was unpopular in Lancashire and Yorkshire because 'Northern players are so bad out of touch that the law was infringed in every instance and scrummages were constantly necessary.' Also, they did not understand 'the finer points [of the game] which distinguish the intelligent player from him who relies on his stamina and physique.'[1]

In 1897, two years after its formation, the Northern Union abolished the line-out 'because it is as a rule an unattractive incident succeeded by a scrimmage, but also because it is a piece of play which is undesirable in a scientific and sportsmanlike sense'. It was replaced by what was known as a punt-out from touch – similar to Sheffield's 1877 proposal to the Football Association – but this too proved to be messy and somewhat dangerous, replaced by a scrum in 1902.

That was not quite the last hurrah for line-outs in league. In 1947, an experiment with a throw-in from touch was tried instead of a scrum when the ball went over the touch-line. This was quickly abandoned after a single unsatisfying trial match between Bramley and the New Zealand tourists.

In rugby union, the line-out continued to be an essential

feature, not least because it allowed teams the opportunity to start a rolling maul and drive their opponents back. This was very much old-school, forward-based British rugby union. But when the 1905 All Blacks arrived they brought a very different conception, in which a line-out was an opportunity to get the ball out to the backs as quickly as possible.

One practical difference this made was that the All Blacks did not use their scrum-half to throw the ball into the line-out. Similar to their philosophy of the scrum, they wanted the scrum-half to receive the ball and swiftly pass it out to the backs, so they gave that role to the hooker.

As with so many things in rugby union in the first half of the 20th century, not much changed until the 1950s. The New Zealanders and Australians largely went their own way and the British and South Africans stuck to their own traditions. The choice to have a line-out or scrum was abolished in 1939 because it was felt the scrum option led to negative tactics.

In the 1950s, a series of rule changes came in to open the game up. This saw the scrum-half role at the line-out changed to become a distributor of the ball rather than the thrower. That was usually done by the nearest winger and became the norm from the 1960s, with perhaps the best known 'throw-in winger' being the great All Black, Grant Batty.

The 1950s also saw the emergence of the modern throw-in style. Demonstrating how football codes borrow from each other, the modern way began with American football half-back Pete Dawkins, who in 1958 won the Heisman Trophy – college football's player of the season – with the Army team. He went to study at Oxford University in 1959 and quickly transferred his skills to become a rugby union winger.

In preparation for the 1959 Varsity match, Oxford captain Malcolm Phillips came up with a fresh tactic, as Dawkins himself recalled: 'In those days wingers threw the ball into

Line-Outs and Throw-Ins: Separated At Birth?

the line-out and most did it underarm. But we had the idea that if I could throw it overarm 40 yards past the forwards at a line-out, it might give our three-quarters an advantage.'[2]

This wasn't quite true. Over-the-shoulder throwing was fairly common, but his torpedo throw revolutionised the line-out. It also eventually meant that the hooker replaced the winger, as the option of a long throw now meant two wingers became an attacking option from the restart.

However as union slowly became commercially reliant on television in the 1970s and 1980s, and moved towards more professional and competitive attitudes, the line-out was seen as a continuing source of problems. It slowed the game down, a den of iniquity full of foul play and technical infringements.

In 1992, feeling a need to speed things up, the International Rugby Board introduced the quick throw-in and, in 1999, a hundred and twenty-odd years of tradition was overthrown when players were finally allowed to lift each other, hitherto the moral equivalent of stealing a chap's homework.

And, as with all set-pieces in both codes of rugby, the importance of the line-out has fallen dramatically since.

According to World Rugby statistics, there were an average of 57 line-outs in international matches in 1983. At the 2021 Six Nations this had more than halved to 26. What's more, the so-called 'struggle for possession' has almost disappeared. In 1983, the throwing side won only around 58 per cent of its line-outs, but in 2021 the ball was retained 89 per cent of the time by the thrower's team.

Whisper it quietly among rugby union people, but the line-out is going the same way as the rugby league scrum.

---

[1] Frank Mitchell, 'Forward Play' in Montague Shearman (ed.), *Football* (London: 1899) pp. 210 & 276.
[2] *Daily Telegraph*, 24 Oct 2007.

15.

Are Leicester Tigers The Most Important Club In The History Of Rugby Union?

Leicester Tigers are one of the biggest and most successful clubs in the history of rugby union. But perhaps its greatest achievement happened over one hundred years ago, when it saved rugby union from the threat of rugby league.

The club was born in a region with a long tradition of folk football. As early as the 14th century, John O'Gaunt is said to have stopped near Leicester to watch a match. Fifteen miles from Leicester, the village of Hallaton has an ancient Easter Monday 'Bottle-Kicking' game that is a remnant of that past.

Organised football in Leicestershire was recorded in local newspapers from at least 1790. In 1829, 'fifteen of Wigston' played fifteen of Blaby for six pounds. In Leicester itself, local printers played Derby printers on Good Friday 1838.

Blaby and Wigston met again in a fifteen-a-side game on Shrove Tuesday, 1852. The next month Leicestershire villages Enderby and Whetstone played each other. Enderby had such

The Most Important Club In The History Of Rugby Union?

a strong reputation they challenged a team from Holmfirth, near Huddersfield, on Good Friday 1852, at the neutral ground of Sheffield's Hyde Park.

So 'football' of different types was deeply embedded in Leicestershire culture. As both rugby and soccer became mass spectator sports from the 1870s, it was rugby that became the most popular code of football in in the county.

This growing popularity was linked to huge economic and social changes taking place across Britain. Between 1861 and 1901, Leicester's population increased from 68,000 to 212,000. The city industrialised and became a world leader in hosiery, textiles and footwear. When workers in most industries were given Saturday afternoons off in 1874, thousands began playing or watching rugby, filling their new-found leisure time and creating a sense of local identity.

The first local rugby clubs we know about were Leicester Athletic and St Margaret's, both founded in 1869. They did not survive, but a decade later, on 3 August 1880 at the George Hotel in the centre of town, Leicester Societies FC, Leicester Amateur FC and Leicester Alert FC joined together to form Leicester Football Club, today's Leicester Tigers.

As in many parts of the Midlands, rugby was the first code of football to become popular. Leicester Fosse (forerunner of Leicester City FC) wasn't formed until 1884. Coventry rugby club was formed in 1874, but Coventry City not until 1883. Nuneaton rugby club was formed in 1879, but Nuneaton Town not until 1889. Northampton Saints were formed in 1880, but Northampton Town not until 1897. In so many Midlands towns, rugby had a head start on soccer.

The 1880s also saw the emergence of dozens of local rugby teams in Leicester, usually based on churches or factories, such as: Excelsior, St Michael's, St Peter's, Belgrave Rovers, Belgrave Premier Works, Anchor, Belgrave Road Old Boys,

Syston Street Old Boys and Belgrave Primitive Methodists. By the end of the century there were five divisions of the local Leicester league, with over 1,000 registered players.

Rugby's appeal was accelerated by the Midlands Counties Cup from 1882. Rivalries between towns and cities could now be played out in the battle for a trophy. In 1888, over 14,000 people watched Burton defeat Coventry in the final, only 5,000 fewer than had attended that year's FA Cup final.

For the first few years, the Midlands Cup was dominated by Moseley in Birmingham. But from 1898 Leicester won it eight times in succession before withdrawing for three years. The Tigers returned in 1909 to win another four times before 1914. The strength of rugby throughout the town could be seen in the fact that even Leicester junior side Stoneygate reached the semi-final in 1906. The 1913 final saw Tigers play local side Belgrave Premier Works (a major shoe factory on Leicester's Melton Road) with the Tigers winning, 39-8.

The popularity of rugby in the town made it commercially very successful. In 1899, Tigers made a profit of £826 on turnover of £3,281, making them one of the richest rugby or soccer clubs in Britain. Competition for the best players led to accusations that they and the junior clubs had a somewhat flexible attitude to the RFU's amateur rules, which banned anyone who received money or other inducements to play.

Suspicions were especially aroused when ace forward Edward Redman moved from top Yorkshire club Manningham in Bradford to the Tigers in 1893 and became the landlord of a local pub, something that northern clubs commonly used as a way of rewarding star players.

William Cail, the president of the RFU and a staunch amateurism advocate told the press that 'Leicester had a bad name for poaching and using undue influence'. But it was not only the Tigers who came under suspicion. Offering jobs

The Most Important Club In The History Of Rugby Union?

and other inducements to players was a widespread, if covert, practice throughout the city's junior clubs. In August 1908, S.A. Austin, secretary of Belgrave FC, complained to the Midland Counties Rugby Union that the rival Premier Works club had illegally offered eight Belgrave players jobs as shoemaking machinists as 'inducement' to join them.

In fact, in terms of popularity and importance to local communities, not to mention the widespread payment of players, the rugby culture of Leicester was much closer to rugby league towns like Hull, Wigan or Leeds than it was to Richmond, Blackheath or Twickenham.

In August 1895, the same month that rugby's great split took place, Leicester appointed Tom Crumbie as their new secretary. A printer and stationer in the town, Crumbie began recruiting the best players to the Tigers. He also set about improving their fixture list, seeking out matches against the top London and Welsh teams. More than anyone else, he was responsible for creating the modern Leicester Tigers.

With the big rugby clubs in the north leaving the RFU, Leicester became the biggest club in English rugby union. Under Crumbie, it operated in the same commercial and competitive way as the rugby league teams in the north of England. When South Shields rugby union club joined rugby league in 1901 rumours began that Leicester would be next.

However, in that same year the RFU announced that Leicester would host an England international match and, in February 1902, England beat Ireland 6-3 in front of 14,000 at Welford Road. Two years later, it staged the England versus Wales match, a 14-14 draw, the only time Wales did not defeat England between 1899 and 1909. In 1906, Ireland were again the visitors, winning 16-6. And in 1909, the Tigers were also granted a match against the Barbarians, a symbolic vote of confidence in the club's loyalty to rugby union.

The staging of international matches at Welford Road not only rewarded the Tigers' loyalty but also consolidated its position as rugby union's strongest club outside of London. In the words of Tom Crumbie, Leicester was 'the first line of defence against the professionalism of the Northern Union.'

But all was not quite as it appeared.

In January 1907, Leicester, along with Coventry and Northampton, were accused of paying players by former England international and Moseley club secretary James Byrne. The RFU's 'Committee on Veiled Professionalism' investigated and reported widespread violations of amateur regulations. These included unaudited accounts, vague balance sheets, expenses paid without receipts, 'unnecessary refreshments' for players, and one case of a player being offered money to stay with the club. But amazingly, the committee concluded 'so far as they could ascertain ... veiled professionalism did not now exist in the Rugby Union game'![1]

The report caused outrage. At the RFU annual general meeting James Byrne asked rhetorically, if there was no veiled professionalism why were Leicester and Northampton told to ask players to refund payments made. Sam Tattersall of Yorkshire asked why Leicester had not been suspended for fielding a former rugby league player – F.S. Jackson, who had played for Swinton and York – an offence for which Yorkshire clubs would be automatically suspended.

In response, the RFU voted down a motion calling for the Tigers to be expelled but announced another inquiry into the accusations. Yet when that inquiry reported back in January 1909, it also cleared the club of all charges. In disgust, RFU president Arnold Crane resigned, complaining the inquiry's findings were 'an encouragement of professionalism rather than an effort to eradicate it'. James Byrne's motion to expel Leicester, Coventry and Northampton from rugby union was

The Most Important Club In The History Of Rugby Union?

defeated by 189 to 11 votes after RFU secretary Rowland Hill stated the impact of the motion 'would be to practically break up the union.'[2]

And he was right. If Leicester were expelled, they had no choice but to join rugby league – and that would have been a mortal blow to the RFU's national authority.

Coventry, Northampton and similar clubs in the Midlands would have followed suit, which would have put clubs in the South West under pressure. Wales yet again would have eventually had their loyalty to the RFU tested.

So the RFU's refusal to apply their amateur laws to Leicester meant threat of another split in English rugby was averted. Leicester remained in rugby union.

Tom Crumbie's belief that Leicester was the first line of defence against the Northern Union was confirmed, but it had been a damned close thing.

---

[1] *Yorkshire Post*, 3 March 1908.
[2] For the full story of this period of crisis in the RFU, see *Rugby's Great Split* (Second edition, Abingdon: 2006), pp. 190-194.

16.

Who Painted The Players Out Of William Wollen's 'The Roses Match'?

'The Roses Match' by William Wollen is perhaps the most famous painting in rugby history. It depicts a rugby union match between Lancashire and Yorkshire in the early 1890s, just before rugby's great split took place in 1895.

The match is in full flow. A Yorkshire player is being tackled but has passed the ball to a player outside of him in the centre position. The action takes place just inside Yorkshire's left touch-line, so a considerable part of a very large crowd can be seen. As well as over twenty contemporary players, the referee, RFU secretary Rowland Hill, and one of the touch judges, Yorkshire Rugby Union official James Miller, are also depicted. Both officials are wearing suits and ties.

Wollen, a well-known artist, was born in 1857. He studied art at Slade and exhibited at the Royal Academy for the first time in 1879. He made his name with contemporary and historic military scenes, very much seen as promoting the

Who Painted The Players Out Of 'The Roses Match'?

spirit of the British Empire. He also illustrated British army campaigns in South Africa for newspapers and magazines and, in World War One, became an official war artist. His work adorned books, most notably Arthur Conan Doyle's *The Exploits of Brigadier Gerard*. In the summer of 1896 'The Roses Match' was exhibited at the Royal Academy, probably the first painting of any football code to be so honoured.

However, 'The Roses Match' is remembered for something entirely different today. It is talked about because it is widely believed that players who later joined the Northern Union in 1895 were painted out. Indeed, if you look closely enough there is one such ghostly figure next to Rowland Hill.

In the same way that Stalin removed Trotsky's image from photographs in the 1930s' Soviet Union, it is widely believed someone in rugby union decided to rewrite history and edit out inconvenient images of the past.

The story was widely believed in union and league. For union, it was just a continuation of its policy of banning and ostracising anyone who had contact with the rival code; for league, another example of establishment discrimination.

The only problem is that the story isn't true. There is indeed a figure who seems to have been painted over near to Rowland Hill, but there is no indication of his identity.

In fact, Wollen made it a feature of the painting that the players were true likenesses of leading players of the time. Contemporary newspaper reports identified all of them, as well as those leading officials seen in the crowd.

The *Huddersfield Chronicle* named 22 players, as well as eight officials in the stand, and said it showed Manningham's Alf Barraclough passing the ball to Bradford's Jack Toothill, just as Oldham's Sam Lees tackles him. Positioned outside Toothill is Bradford's Tommy Dobson. Bradford's Fred Cooper is tangled up with Oldham's Bill McCutcheon and

Heckmondwike's Dicky Lockwood.[1] All of these would join the Northern Union in 1895, and so would pretty much every other player thus rendered. What's more, the painting was exhibited in the north of England during the autumn and winter of 1895, immediately after the formation of the NU, so anyone painted out would have immediately been spotted by journalists, or indeed the public who paid sixpence each to go and view it.

Therefore the story that Wollen painted out a Northern Union player cannot be true. Indeed, if all those who joined the Northern Union had been painted out, there would barely have been anyone left on the canvas!

But the painting does have mysteries to be unravelled.

Why paint it in the first place? A leaf through Wollen's catalogue seems to indicate that this is the only rugby picture he ever did. There is no evidence that he was a rugby fan, and even if he was, why would he paint a Lancashire versus Yorkshire game rather than an England international match?

Wollen was actually commissioned to paint the picture by a company called 'Mawson, Swan and Morgan' of Newcastle. Joseph Swan was one of Britain's leading scientists, inventor of the light bulb and a method of developing photographs. Together with partners John Mawson and Thomas Morgan, he owned a large shop on Grey Street in the middle of Newcastle selling stationery, books, photographic equipment and much more. It even had a fine art department. It was one of the city's leading retailers from the late 19th century until it finally closed down in 1986.

We don't know why the company funded the painting. It's possible that one or more of the partners was a rugby fan. Until the late 1880s, Newcastle was seen as a rugby city, and rugby union retained great support among the local middle classes even after the North East became a hotbed of soccer.

Above: William Wollen's mysterious painting 'The Battle of the Roses'

Left: The only known image of William Webb Ellis

J. ANDERTON. T. KENT. W. BUMBY. A. SHREWSBURY. H. BROOKS. J. LAWLOR. T. BANKS. A. SAUL.
A. S. LAING. J. SMITH. W. H. THOMAS. C. MATHERS. A. PINKETH. W. BURNETT. R. L. SEDDON.

H. C. SPEAKMAN. S. WILLIAMS. J. NOLAN. A. E. STODDART. J. T. HASLAM. R. BURNETT. H. EAGLES.
A. J. STUART. J. G. McSHANE.

Above: Not the First Lions – Shaw & Shrewsbury's 1888 Rugby Touring Team

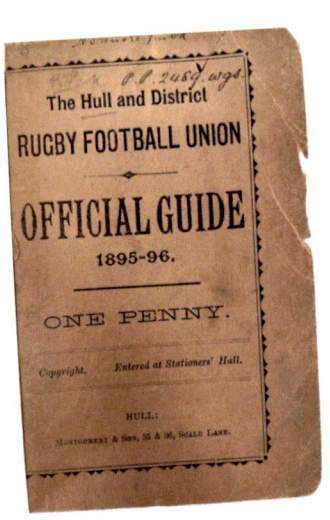

Above: The Hull & District Rugby *Official Guide* for 1895

Right: Lucius Banks – from the collection of M. Tyler Radabaugh (like Lucius, a Middlesex County, Virginia native)

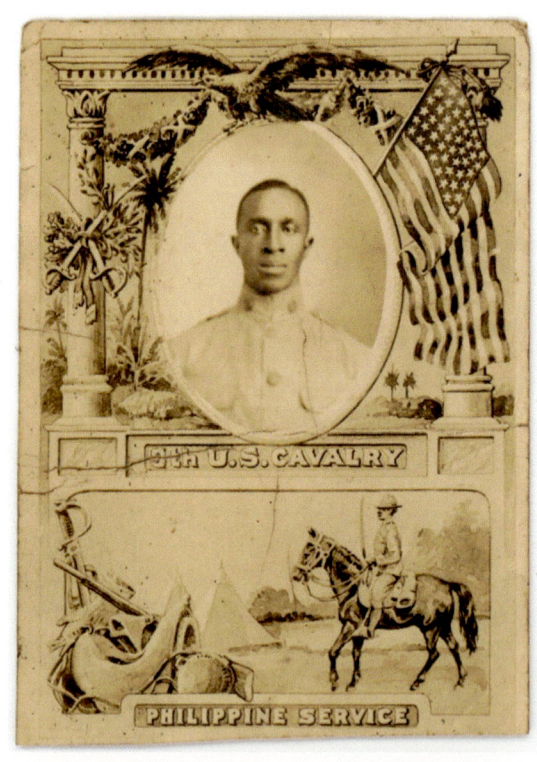

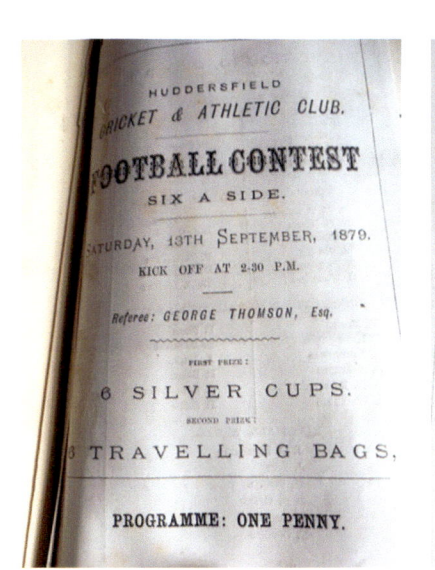

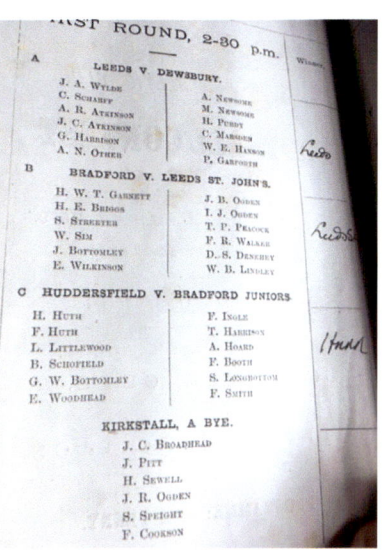

Above: Is this the first ever limited player rugby tournament? Huddersfield six-a-side from 1879

Left: Robert Delaunay's painting, 'L'Equipe de Cardiff', of 1913

Above: Workington's Dearham Amazons women's rugby league team of 1953
(*Image courtesy of Victoria Dawson*)

Above: Poster for *This Sporting Life* – not just a film about rugby

Who Painted The Players Out Of 'The Roses Match'?

'The Roses Match' was exhibited in the shop's art gallery in December 1898.

But why choose Lancashire versus Yorkshire? After all, the Northumberland v Durham county match was still one of the highlights of the local season. It's possible that the painting was intended to be a marketing tool in the industrial counties to the south. Most newspaper reports about it mention the company's name, and the combination of famous artist and famous players would have been a forerunner of today's sponsorship of art exhibitions by the likes of Shell and BP.

Newspaper reports also highlight another intriguing issue. Rugby historians, including myself, have always believed that the painting shows the 1893 Roses match at Bradford's Park Avenue ground. Indeed, a lot of work was spent identifying the players to reach this conclusion.

However, the digitisation of newspapers, especially by the British Newspaper Archive, has meant that historians can now do far deeper research than was ever possible in the days of physical paper and microfilm. By tracking local reports of the artwork, we now know that its original title was not 'The Roses Match' but the more exciting 'The Battle of the Roses'.

Just as interesting, newspapers are quite clear that it does not depict an actual match but is a general representation. As the *Manchester Advertiser* pointed out, it is the equivalent of a composite photo, its reporter noting that Dicky Lockwood and Fred Cooper, both prominently depicted, never played together in the same Yorkshire team.

This is not the only revelation digitised newspapers have revealed. Far from depicting Bradford's Park Avenue, papers all agree that the venue is Manchester's Fallowfield Grounds, later Fallowfield Stadium, which staged 1892's Roses Match.

Opened that same year, Fallowfield became famous in 1893 when it staged the FA Cup final between Wolves and

Everton that attracted a record 45,000 spectators, almost triple its official capacity. It also hosted the NU Challenge Cup final in 1899 and 1900. A close comparison of the layouts of Fallowfield and Park Avenue confirms the painting's setting.

After its exhibition at Mawson, Swan and Morgan's Newcastle gallery in 1898, it seems to have disappeared. This is somewhat strange given the high profile William Wollen enjoyed until his death in 1936. It could have been forgotten about, often the case with art, or its depiction of numerous NU players meant it had become slightly embarrassing.

It reappeared in 1957, apparently purchased in an antiques shop in Grey Street, which happens to be where Mawson, Swan and Morgan leased property from 1935. It is possible therefore that the painting was stored away and then sold on to an antiques shop because no-one realised what it was.

We don't know who bought it, but it ended up on the wall of the clubhouse of Otley rugby club in Yorkshire. And it was from there that the story of the paintings-out emerged.

There is of course one final mystery. That player standing near the referee who has been painted over – why?

The reason is probably perfectly innocent. As anyone who has watched TV programmes like *Britain's Lost Masterpieces* will know, it is very common for artists to alter compositions and move subjects around on the canvas. Perhaps an over-zealous cleaner rubbed too much dirt away and inadvertently took off a layer of paint to reveal Wollen's original layout?

We will never know. But we certainly do know that he was not removed because he joined the Northern Union.

Once again, 'The Battle of the Roses' highlights rugby's unfailing ability to mine myths from half-remembered history.

---

[1] *Huddersfield Chronicle*, 24 Jan 1896.

17.

Why Scrums Aren't What They Used To Be (But Never Were Anyway)

Every so often you hear people call for a return to 'proper scrums', but the truth is there has never really been a time when 'proper scrums' existed.

In fact, the scrum is even older than rugby itself. It was an essential part of those pre-industrial mass football games referred to earlier, played between villages or districts, like the annual Ashbourne Shrovetide match, where men (and occasionally women) struggled endlessly in their hundreds for possession of the ball.

The scrum was also a vital part of the different types of football at English public schools in the mid-19th century, from which modern soccer and rugby are directly descended. For example, the Eton wall game resembles a continuous scrum played against a wall. At Winchester, where its game is often seen as a predecessor of soccer, the scrum, known as a 'hot', is also a central part of the activity.

At Rugby School, the game revolved around scrummaging and kicking to set up scrums. As in soccer, forwards were the attacking players. Their aim was to push the scrum back to their opponents' goal or to break through the opposing pack and dribble the ball forward. Backs were defensive players, whose role was to defend the goal or kick the ball downfield to set up another scrum.

When the English Rugby Football Union was formed 1871, it amended Rugby School's rules. Teams were twenty-a-side, of which as many as fifteen players were forwards. A scrum was formed every time a player with the ball was tackled to the ground. He would be allowed to get up, then the forwards of both sides would form a scrum around him.

RFU secretary Arthur Guillemard described how it all worked in those days. When the ball-carrier was brought to the ground with a tackle: 'the forwards of each side hurry up and a scrummage is instantly formed, each ten facing their opponents' goal, packed round the ball, shoulder to shoulder, leg to leg, as tight as they can stand, the twenty thus forming a round compact mass with the ball in the middle.'[1]

The tackled player then placed the ball on the ground, shouted 'Down', and both sets of forwards started to push. Their object was to move the ball forward and push through the opposing pack. Heeling it out of the scrum was felt to be a form of cheating.

England forward Charles Gurdon remembered how scrums sometimes lasted ten minutes in the 1870s because forwards pushed endlessly against each other to force the ball through their opponents. As you might imagine, this was not a game for spectators, and by 1875 reforms were demanded. As the sporting weekly *Bell's Life* asked: 'How much longer are we to be wearied by monotonous shoving matches?' To improve the game for players and spectators, in 1876 the RFU

Why Scrums Aren't What They Used To Be

decided that international matches would be played fifteen-a-side, and rugby at all levels soon followed suit.

This marked the start of almost two decades of radical reforms. Fifteen-a-side meant fewer forwards and smaller scrums that no longer lasted for minutes, because it was easier for the ball to come out. Most importantly, teams began to heel the ball out deliberately.

In 1878 the RFU decided that a tackled player now had to let go of the ball immediately. This meant that forwards now had to keep up with the play, expanding the available space on the field, and creating more opportunities for the backs.

The impact of these changes was famously seen in 1882, when a team from the West Yorkshire mining village Thornes won the Yorkshire Cup thanks to their revolutionary scrum tactics of protecting their scrum-half with a wing-forward, heeling the ball quickly out and allocating specific scrum positions to their forwards. Thornes' tactics anticipated the 1905 All Blacks by a generation.

Many such changes were not welcomed by traditionalists. RFU president Arthur Budd even argued that heeling the ball out of the scrum should be made illegal, because it put the forwards in front of the ball in an offside position.

Others thought the changes did not go far enough. Yorkshire Rugby Union president James Miller's 1892 call for the game to be thirteen-a-side was based on his belief that what he called rugby's 'Pushing Age' was over and forwards should be reduced from eight to six to speed up the game.

So immediately after the rugby split in 1895, the Northern Union discussed moving to six forwards in thirteen-a-side teams. But the change was initially voted down, and over the next decade the number of scrums grew dramatically. In 1899, to get rid of messy rucks and mauls, the Northern Union introduced a rule that if a tackled player could not release the ball, a scrum had to be formed. Although this tidied up the tackle it hugely increased the amount of scrummaging. This led to games like Hunslet's 1902 match against Halifax, when there were 110 of the things. Ironically, the set scrum now had more importance in league than in union.

Eventually, in June 1906, the problem was solved when teams were reduced to thirteen-a-side and no more than six forwards on each team were allowed to pack down. At the same time, the NU introduced a modified version of the RFU's 1871 rule. The tackled ball carrier was allowed to stand up, put the ball down in front in front of him and play it with his foot. The 'play-the-ball' was conceived as a sort of mini-scrum, and it wasn't until the early 1990s that the defending player, the marker, was stopped from trying to play the ball.

In contrast, the rugby union scrum after 1895 remained largely unchanged. It only began to evolve again with the arrival of touring teams from the Southern Hemisphere in the mid-1900s. The 1906 Springbok tourists brought their own tactical innovations. They packed down in a 3-4-1 formation – three in the front row, four in the second and a single back-row forward. This meant the scrum could be wheeled around more easily to attack. The two flankers in the second row and back rower (the modern number eight) could quickly detach to attack or to snuff out opposing moves from the scrum.

The New Zealanders had a completely different approach, using a 2-3-2 formation, with a free-standing eighth wing-forward, who fed the scrum and shielded the scrum-half, who stood behind the back row to allow quicker passing from the base. Many in England thought the All Blacks' wing-forward was unsportsmanlike if not downright illegal.

The controversy came to a head on the 1930 British Isles tour to Australasia. British manager James Baxter suggested that Cliff Porter, the All Black wing-forward and captain, was

Why Scrums Aren't What They Used To Be

a cheat. As soon as Baxter returned home, he persuaded the RFU to effectively outlaw the wing-forward and 2-3-2 scrum.

Ironically, the England national side that won four grand slams in the 1920s played a power forward game inspired by the All Blacks. Its architect was English captain William Wavell Wakefield, who built his teams on back-rowers who could cover every inch of ground both in defence and attack.

But by the mid-1930s matches were dominated by defensive back-row play and try-scoring dried up. Arguably the low point came with the 1931 Springbok tour to Britain. They perfected a game plan of 'touch-kick-scrum-touch-kick' ad infinitum.

Union continued to be oppressed by forward domination and kicking in the 1950s. BBC commentator G.V. Wynne-Jones called for the number of forwards to be reduced to six. The International Rugby Board altered scrum rules regularly but, far from opening it up, they added to the complexity.

Despite its reputation for thrilling flair, French rugby union felt it had no choice but to adopt the scrummaging game in the 1950s. Frustrated by its failure to win the Five Nations, France finally found success in 1959 by emulating English forward play, rather than by open rugby. As the great French rugby writer Denis Lalanne wrote: 'We know where rugby begins and where it must begin all over again. It certainly does not begin in the back row. It begins in the *front row*.'[2] This was taken to heart and the great French Grand Slam-winning teams of the 1960s and 1970s were based on the same principal of forward power.

However, the advent of professionalism in union gave rise to new problems that would undermine the scrum. The professional era renewed union's evolutionary impulse. The impact of commercialism took it down the road rugby league had travelled and changes were made to improve the game as a spectacle, from legalising lifting in the line-out to changing the ruck and maul, chasing more continuous play. The scrum came under particular scrutiny, and its importance to the game has since diminished.

Rugby union is now faced with a paradox. The symbolism of the scrum has increased while many of the sport's other cherished traditions, such as amateurism, have gone. The supercharged collision of two front rows to begin the scrum is itself a new phenomenon, unknown to earlier front rows, which emphasises how it is now a ritual in decline.

World Rugby's statistics show that the average number of scrums in the 2021 Six Nations was ten per match – roughly the same as in rugby league – down from around 40 in the 1970s. And, as we have seen, the 'contest for possession' is also declining in importance.

In short, the union scrum is going the way of league's, which has also solved the problem of the breakdown by replacing the ruck and the maul with the play-the-ball. Excessive touch kicking was curbed by penalising direct kicking into touch.

As professionalism and victory became paramount, league discovered, as union is today, that players and coaches always find a way to circumvent rules. This led to the gradual abandonment of the struggle for possession and a reduction in the scrum's importance in the 1990s. In its place, league has evolved largely into a struggle for territory and position.

The scrum will not die. Rugby of both codes is too rooted in its traditions, culture and belief systems. But its importance will whither, until it becomes, like the human coccyx, an almost redundant vestigial reminder of the evolutionary past.

---

[1] 'The Rugby Union Game With Hints to Players', in Thomas P. Power (ed.) *The Footballer* (Melbourne: 1877), p. 11.
[2] Denis Lalanne, *The Great Fight of the French Fifteen* (Wellington: 1960) p. 200.

18.

Leeds United's Secret Rugby League History

Since the 1960s, Leeds United have been one of English soccer's most iconic clubs. Don Revie's years as manager transformed the team from a middling first division side into a contender for Europe's highest honours.

But none of what Revie and his successors achieved would have been possible without a rugby league match played on 14 May 1904, the day the history of the club we know today as Leeds United truly began.

It was then that Holbeck lost 7-0 to St Helens.

Such a defeat wouldn't normally be a significant date for the history books, but this was a play-off between the second and third-placed teams in rugby league's second division, the prize being promotion to the first. Both Holbeck and Saints finished on 49 points, the latter finishing second due to a better points difference.

The game was at Huddersfield and, as might be expected

with so much at stake, was a tight, dour affair. St Helens wore Holbeck down, scoring a single try and a couple of goals to clinch a spot in the following year's top flight.

Even so, it wasn't a bad end to the campaign for Holbeck. The south Leeds team had been on an upward trajectory over the last few seasons. Fourteenth in the second tier four years previously, they climbed to fifth in the next two before reaching the brink of promotion.

The future seemed bright.

The club had been formed to play rugby on Holbeck Recreation Ground, which in the 1870s was Leeds's major sports arena, hosting Yorkshire county cricket matches and the first-ever Yorkshire Cup final in 1877.

By the late 1880s, Holbeck were one of the leading rugby clubs in the city. Alongside Leeds, Hunslet and Bramley, it was a founder member of the Leeds & District Rugby Union in 1888. A year later, it was investigated by the Yorkshire Rugby Union for helping to buy a wedding present for its star player George Broadbent, which was, bizarrely, a violation of rugby's amateur regulations.

At 1891's RFU AGM, it was Holbeck who proposed future meetings should alternate between venues north and south, instead of in London, which usually guaranteed a majority for whatever the RFU leadership wanted.

The club joined the Northern Union in 1896, part of the second wave of teams attracted by the success of the NU in its first year. But it struggled in rugby league, hemmed in by the success of Hunslet and rarely finishing above the other three professional Leeds clubs.

Even so, they had prominent local supporters, not least Joe Henry, owner of Leeds's largest iron foundry and prominent member of the local Liberal Party, who would become Lord Mayor in 1918. Hopeful for the future, in January 1897 the club announced it was buying land from Bentley's Brewery to build a new ground near the Peacock Inn on Elland Road.

To purchase the Elland Road site, the club converted itself into Holbeck Football and Athletic Club Limited, and issued 2,000 shares valued at one pound each to buy the land for eleven hundred pounds. In order to safeguard their own interests and that of the brewery, a clause was inserted in the purchase agreement specifying that rugby had to be played at the ground for at least the next seven years, and that the brewery would have sole rights to provide refreshments.[1]

At Holbeck's first annual meeting in July 1898, Joe Henry, now the club chairman and one of three councillors on the board of directors, announced it had made a healthy profit, that the ground was an appreciating asset, and the council had agreed to build a direct tram line from the city that would pass through Elland Road. But in its first few Northern Union seasons Holbeck struggled for success, bumping along the bottom of the league until the early 1900s.

At the same time, soccer was growing in popularity, especially in South Leeds. In a city saturated with rugby, Hunslet was the base for one of its first soccer clubs, Hunslet Association FC, which had been formed in 1877. Rugby and soccer vied for popularity there until the mid-1880s, when the rise of Hunslet rugby club cemented oval ball popularity.

Nevertheless, support for soccer remained strong in the district, and the national prominence of the FA Cup and the Football League offered an attractive alternative.

By 1904 the 86 soccer clubs in the Leeds district outnumbered amateur rugby league clubs. As well as rugby, Elland Road regularly hosted soccer and was the usual venue for the final of the West Yorkshire Cup, the region's most prestigious tournament. Reflecting soccer's following in South Leeds, Hunslet AFC were the leading soccer side of the period, dominating that competition. Even so, the financial demands of running even a local side successfully were difficult to meet, and the club collapsed in 1902 because they were unable to find a suitable ground on which to play.

It was at this point that the fates of rugby and football became entwined. Despite Holbeck having its most successful season ever in the Northern Union, its failure to win promotion in the 1904 play-off match was used by its directors as an excuse to close it down.

They blamed the decision on poor crowds and high player wages but, as one Holbeck supporter pointed out, this was nothing new. 'We know we have had very bad luck in gates last season, but in the past we have been in the same predicament and have succeeded in extricating ourselves from it.' He explained to the *Yorkshire Evening Post* that:

> ...myself, along with others, have been surprised that no special effort seems to have been made by the officials to avoid what seems to the the inevitable break-up of the club... They, frankly, seem to be content to sink into oblivion without any special effort to avoid it.[2]

This didn't appear to be too far from the truth. The loss of £498 was large but not unmanageably so, especially given the fact the club owned its own ground. Moreover, chances of promotion next season looked promising, taking into account the growing success of the team and the weakness of the two relegated teams, Keighley and Huddersfield, neither of whom finished in the promotion places in 1905.

But there was something else going on.

Six weeks after Holbeck's final match, the committee of disbanded Hunslet AFC met and voted to change the club's name to Leeds City Association Football Club. Then, two weeks before the new season kicked off, the Holbeck committee announced that they would ask their players 'to play for next to nothing.'[3]

Needless to say, this meant that most players left and the club directors used that to complain about a lack of loyalty.

A few days later, on 2 September, it was announced that the new Leeds City soccer club, which, as Hunslet, hadn't played a match in two years, had approached the Holbeck committee with an offer to rent or purchase their ground.

Holbeck's officials needed no persuading, proclaiming themselves 'so disgusted with the turn of affairs [of players leaving] that they offered their ground outright to the officials of the newly-formed Leeds City association club.'[4]

A day later it was announced that Leeds City was going to convert itself into a limited liability company in order to purchase Holbeck's ground, which it eventually did for £4,500, and the *Yorkshire Post* declared 'the death knell' for Holbeck rugby club.

It shouldn't have been surprising that the *Yorkshire Post* was keen to write them off. Its leading football writer was A.W. Pullin, who wrote about cricket under the pseudonym 'Old Ebor' and sat on the Leeds City committee.

Holbeck never played another game after the play-off match against St Helens in May. But in September 1905, Leeds City – the forerunner of Leeds United – kicked off its first match in Football League Division 2.

Professional soccer had finally come to Leeds.

You don't have to be a conspiracy theorist to recognise the powerful coincidences involved in the demise of Holbeck, not least the fact that the club's 1897 agreement to purchase Elland Road specified that rugby must be played on the ground for at least seven years.

In other words, rugby had to be played until 1904, the

same year the club was shut down. After that, it was straightforward to move a soccer club in.

What's more, the first chairman of Leeds City was also the man who steered the purchase of Elland Road from the rugby club, Joe Henry, who also just happened to be the chairman of Holbeck rugby club.

All of which only goes to prove that just because you are paranoid, it doesn't mean they are not out to get you...

---

[1] For an account of Elland Road's rugby history, see Trevor Delaney's wonderful *The Grounds of Rugby League* (Keighley: 1991).
[2] *Yorkshire Evening Post*, 3 Sept 1904.
[3] *Yorkshire Evening Post*, 20 Aug 1904.
[4] *Yorkshire Evening Post*, 3 Sept 1904.

19.

Why Doesn't Robert Delaunay's Painting 'The Cardiff Team' Show The Cardiff Team?

It's probably true to say that rugby isn't normally associated with modern art or experimental painting. William Wollen's 'The Battle for the Roses' is its more typical traditional style. But in France before the First World War, rugby was part of an exciting new world of science, speed and the avant-garde.

One of the best known examples is Robert Delaunay's 1913 modernist masterpiece, 'The Cardiff Team'. It depicts a player leaping to catch a ball in a line-out. Three opposing players are waiting for him to land, as a team-mate prepares to take the pass. But this is not merely a depiction of match action.

Behind the catcher one can see the Eiffel Tower, a huge Ferris Wheel built for the great Paris Exhibition of 1900, some trees and a bi-plane high in the sky. There are also fragments of text from an advert for an aero-manufacturing company, newspapers and even an advertising hoarding for the artist himself. The painting itself is largely composed with a series of rectangles, using contrasting colours and overlapping perspectives.

First exhibited in February 1913, Delaunay painted several versions of 'The Cardiff Team', the last in 1922. Today you can see different versions in various galleries, including in the Scottish National Gallery of Modern Art in Edinburgh. Use of geometric shapes, shifting perspectives and diverse images position the painting as part of the Cubist movement that had recently emerged in Europe.[1]

Delaunay himself did not like the Cubist description, and his structure of 'The Cardiff Team' is much looser and freer than Albert Gleizes's rigorously Cubist depiction of rugby players, 'The Footballers'. Delaunay preferred to call his art 'Simultaneism', to describe how 'modern sensibilities converge simultaneously.'

Unlike in Britain, where sporting art was so conservative, European artists embraced the spectacle of mass spectator sport. It wasn't until the inter-war years that Christopher Nevinson and Sybil Andrews started to engage with it. But in Europe, mass spectator sport was part of the sudden appearance of modernity, technology and the urban society of the masses in the years before the First World War. While Delaunay was working on 'The Cardiff Team', Italian artist Umberto Boccioni was painting 'Dynamism of a footballer', reflecting the Futurists' fascination with sport.

For European artists, sport was part of what the art critic Robert Hughes later called the 'shock of the new', a feeling captured by other modernist painters such as Jean Metzinger's 'At the Cycle Track', Picasso's 'Footballers on the Beach' and Willi Baumeister's 'Football Player'.

In France, rugby captured the imagination of a number of its leading modernists. In 1908, Henri Rousseau produced the playful and highly mannered 'The Football Players', a strange

Why Doesn't 'The Cardiff Team' Show The Cardiff Team?

dreamlike portrayal of four rugby players competing against each other in a wood. Albert Gleizes produced his sharply geometric 'The Footballers' in 1913 and André Lhote painted a number of depictions of rugby during the same period. In 1913, critic Jacques Rivière and his brother-in-law novelist Alain-Fournier formed the Young Writers Sports Club, which brought together rugby fans from the literary and art worlds. To young French intellectuals, rugby epitomised modernity. Fast, complex, physically and intellectually challenging, the game's British origins also gave it the cachet of the industrial society that still dominated the world.

So Delaunay's painting combined a feeling for these new times with a statement about the new ways of seeing that art was now exploring. 'The Cardiff Team' depicts a world in which the viewer is looking up – to the player leaping for the ball, the ferris wheel taking tourists high above the streets, the Eiffel Tower and the aeroplane taking humanity into the heavens. There are new horizons, their possibilities endless.

But there are also a number of mysteries about Delaunay's painting. Where are the spectators, for example? Matches in France before the First World War commonly attracted four-figure crowds, yet not a single spectator is seen. Delaunay portrays an individual gaze, a single perspective of the event rather than collective vision, which was true of most modernist painters, many of whom disliked the idea of mass society. And rugby union leaders in Britain and France also disparaged that idea, emphasising how theirs was a sport for players rather than watchers. As an upper-class Frenchman, Delaunay may well have shared their distaste for the crowd.

But why is it called 'The Cardiff Team'? Modernist sport paintings were almost self-consciously anonymous, with titles such as the 'The Footballers', 'The Football Players' and, for those who like variation, 'The Rugby Players'.

The answer is because Cardiff represented the modern age – in society and rugby. Cardiff in 1913 was at the cutting edge. It was at the heart of the world's coal trade, a seemingly ever-expanding metropolis that in barely two generations had grown from a population of 25,000 to almost a quarter of a million. Journalists called it 'the Chicago of Wales'.

In 1907, the French writer Joseph Rogues de Fursac had authored an influential book on Wales which investigated the great religious revival that had swept through the country in 1904 and 1905. Commissioned by the French ministry of the interior, it examined the tension between modern secularism and religion, and how Wales had emerged from what Fursac saw as the threat of mysticism. For France, intent on upholding secular principles, the experience of Wales seemed to offer valuable lessons and they were not lost on modernist painters creating art based on science and technology.

And when it came to sport, which in pre-First World War France meant cycling and rugby – soccer did not become a mass spectator sport until after the war – Wales also led the way. It had dominated the Five Nations since 1900, the only northern hemisphere team to have beaten the All Blacks. Most importantly, the Welsh played the most exciting and 'scientific' brand of free-flowing rugby union. And by the time Delaunay was painting 'The Cardiff Team' a significant number of Welshmen were involved in the French game.

In 1907, Welshman James Crockwell had been instrumental in developing the free-running style of Section Paloise, the famous club at the foot of the Pyrenees. In 1909, Welsh fly-half and Cardiff captain Percy Bush was made British consul at Nantes and, not coincidentally, played for the local rugby club, for whom he scored 54 points in one match in 1910. Stade Bordelais became embroiled in controversy when their Welsh coach, William Priest, openly tried to recruit players

Why Doesn't 'The Cardiff Team' Show The Cardiff Team?

from Wales and Scotland. Priest was so blatant that the French rugby union authorities forced the club to sack him. This did not deter the Bordelais who, in 1912, signed 'Billy Bordeaux', otherwise known as William Morgan, brother of Teddy Morgan who scored the Welsh try that beat the 1905 All Blacks. In Paris, George Yewlett coached Stade Français.

But perhaps the most influential Welshman in France in that era was Aviron Bayonnais's Harry Owen Roe of Penarth. In 1912, he broke Aviron's try-scoring record but it was as the player-coach that he made the most impact as architect of the 'La Manière Bayonnaise' (the Bayonne Way), a style of play in which he said 'all players are three-quarters'. Roe's team swept all before them and won the French championship in 1913. Indeed, the tradition of free-flowing French rugby owed much to those Welshmen who 'went south' in the 1900s.

The Cardiff club itself was a regular visitor to Paris, playing showpiece matches there in 1906, 1908 and 1912. The 1906 match took place just a month after the All Blacks had defeated France 38-8 in their first-ever match there. The Welsh club played against the French national team and, captained by Percy Bush, Cardiff won by an equally impressive 27-5. In the 1908 and 1912 matches Cardiff defeated Stade Francais comfortably. So for a Parisian like Robert Delaunay, the embodiment of this rugby modernism was the Cardiff team.

Did Robert Delaunay see any of these matches? One of the mysteries surrounding his painting is that neither team is wearing the colours of Cardiff. What's more, the positioning of the players resembles a photograph of a match between Toulouse and the University Sporting Club in January 1913, so there is no obvious representation of the Cardiff club at all.

But looking for a direct link to a single match is too literal-minded. It doesn't matter if Delaunay went to a match or not. After all, Picasso was not present in Guernica to paint his masterpiece of the terrible events there, and Théodore Géricault did not have to be shipwrecked in the Atlantic to be able to paint 'The Raft of the Medusa'.

Delaunay was not painting a literal representation of a match but using rugby as a metaphor for a world changing so rapidly it can no longer be understood using traditional methods. It is difficult for us in the 21st century to appreciate how new, unusual and exciting modern sport appeared to Europeans in the early 1900s. Less than thirty years earlier, it did not exist.

Rugby, with its combinations and teamwork, its speed, its passing, kicking and tackling, seemed to symbolise the collectivity and new interconnectedness of daily life in an industrial, urban society. Like modern art, and especially Cubism from which Delaunay's art was derived, rugby was all about angles, motion, overlapping images, and differing but simultaneous perspectives.

'The Cardiff Team' is rightly regarded as a major work of French modern art. For the first time, Delaunay is portraying the multiple perspectives of a match from the viewpoint of one spectator. At a match, our vision does not simply consist of two teams, which is how most paintings depict sport. The spectator sees many things simultaneously ... advertising hoardings ... newspapers ... landmarks and buildings ... and most obviously the skyline and sky itself.

As every spectator knows, going to a match is a multi-sensory, multi-dimensional experience where, in Delaunay's words, 'modern sensibilities converge simultaneously.'

Which is why 'The Cardiff Team' is the most important work of art to have ever depicted rugby.

---

[1] For a detailed discussion of the painting see Bernard Vere, *Sport and Modernism in the Visual Arts*, c. 1909-1939 (Manchester: 2018).

20.

Why Are There So Many Penalty Goals In Rugby Union?

Of all ball-based team sports, rugby union is unique in the importance of the penalty to the result. In union's ten World Cup finals since that tournament began in 1987, sixty-four penalty goals have been scored but only twenty-one tries. In only one final, New Zealand's 8-7 win over France in 2011, were more tries than penalties scored.

But why did the penalty goal acquire such an importance?

Its predominance sharply differentiates rugby union from all other varieties of football.

In rugby league, union's closest cousin, the value and importance of the penalty goal was reduced in 1897, just two years after the split that created the two codes.

In American, Australian and Canadian football, early offshoots from the original code of rules based on the game played at Rugby School, the penalty goal concept does not exist.

Only in soccer does the penalty play an important role in determining the result of a match, but this is due to the low-scoring nature of the sport, in which a single goal can determine the outcome, rather than the frequency with which the penalty goal itself is scored.

This is not merely a quirk of rugby union's scoring system. Many reformers have campaigned – and indeed continue to campaign – for a reduction in the value of a penalty goal. In 1955, even the former England captain and president of the RFU, William Wavell Wakefield, complained that 'there are too many penalty goals scored in most games.'[1]

The dissidents who formed the rugby league code argued before the 1895 split for the primacy of try-scoring over goal-kicking. Yet the union authorities have steadfastly refused to reduce the value of a penalty. Despite union raising the value of a try to four points in 1971, and five points in 1992, the penalty goal remains a crucial way of deciding a match, especially in important games like the World Cup final.

Its dominance is not just a technical feature but a reflection of the sport's history and culture.

Rugby union was a creation of the mid-Victorian British middle-classes, who sought order and hierarchy in their relationships with society's other, lowlier, classes. To maintain this, its leaders developed an elaborate code of behaviour and extensive structure of sanctions against those who they felt transgressed their values and rules. Fear of the penalty, both off and on the field, became one of the game's defining characteristics.

The introduction of the penalty, and subsequently penalty goal, was part of the process by which the leadership of the RFU sought to control those they felt were alien influences.

In the first decades of rugby's history, when the game was confined to young men educated at universities and British

Why Are There So Many Penalty Goals In Rugby Union?

public schools, the control of matches attracted little discussion. Even after the formation of the RFU in 1871, games were conducted according to the players' appreciation of the purpose of the game and shared social backgrounds. Disputes were resolved by discussions between opposing captains. It was not until 1874 that the rules of rugby even referred to the control of a match.

'The captains of the respective sides shall be the sole arbiters of all disputes,' the RFU's newly amended Law Six stated. By the mid-1870s it had become the custom for each side to provide an umpire, who would be the first resort if a dispute over rules occurred. As in cricket, from which the idea had been borrowed, the umpire could only intervene if a player made a direct appeal to him about a breach of the rules.

Until 1882, there was no mention of punishment if rules were broken. At Rugby School and some rugby clubs in the 1860s, it was the custom to allow the non-offending side a hack below the knee against someone who transgressed. The ban on hacking in the RFU's first set of rules in 1871 seems to have led to a scrum being formed when a breach occurred, but again this was due to an unwritten but mutually understood code of behaviour.

This system of regulation through informal agreement broke down in the 1880s, as the appeal of the game spread far beyond the privately-educated middle classes. A massive increase in the number of working class players in the game was acknowledged in the 1880 edition of *The Football Annual* by RFU secretary Arthur Guillemard, who pointed out that 'the recent foundation of a large number of clubs in the North has resulted in the drafting into club XVs of a large proportion of tyros, who may know how to drop and place kick, but are unlearned in the various points of the game.'[2]

Although initially welcomed, the popularity of the sport among the industrial working class was soon viewed with concern by RFU leaders. 'It is an open question whether this interest has not been attained at the expense of our noble sport', pondered RFU secretary Rowland Hill in *The Football Annual* of 1882.[3] By the mid-1880s, there was widespread fear that working-class participation was driving out middle-class players.

In response to these concerns, the RFU began to shift control of matches out of the hands of the players. In 1881 it decreed that umpires should be neutrals rather than representatives of the two teams. In 1885, a referee had to be appointed to a match with the mutual consent of both teams.

At this time, the role of the referee was mainly confined to arbitrating on disagreements between the two umpires but, crucially, he could intervene in cases of violent play or players disputing the officials' decisions. In 1889, the RFU gave the referee power to send-off any player disputing his decisions. Thus two of the great fears of the middle-class player – being subject to violence from those he believed socially inferior, and the questioning of his authority – were addressed.

As part of this new system of regulation, in 1882 the RFU also amended the rules to allow a free kick to be awarded for offside. This initially took the form of a punt or a drop-kick, and the rules explicitly stated that 'no goal could be scored from it'. The free-kick penalty was gradually applied to other offences, but it was only in 1886 that a place-kick could be taken as a penalty and a goal scored directly from it. In 1892, the rule was extended so that penalty kicks could be awarded for all infringements.

The penalty goal was now written into the rules.

The same fears that had resulted in the rules of the game being rewritten were also seen in the debate about payments

Why Are There So Many Penalty Goals In Rugby Union?

to working-class players. Until 1886, the RFU had no rules relating to amateurism or professionalism. But as great crowds flocked to matches in the industrial north of England, it became an open secret that leading working-class players received covert remuneration. At its October 1886 general meeting, the RFU banned all forms of payment to players, with the explicit aim of thwarting working-class influence.

The introduction of the penalty goal on the field and the imposition of amateurism off it were both aspects of the RFU's system of discipline and punishment. This link between the introduction of the penalty and the perceived threat to RFU authority was summed up by Scottish journalist RJ Phillips in his 1925 history of Scottish rugby: 'Professionalism had already become a disturbing element, and irregularities on the field had increased. The penalty goal was an English repressive, and was intended as a corrective of prevalent abuses.'[4]

Over the past decade, the changes to union rules have seen something of a reduction in the importance of penalty goals. Statistics from World Rugby show that the 2017 Six Nations was the last in which penalty goals outnumbered tries. But if we take perennial wooden-spooners Italy out of the equation, the 2021 and 2022 tournaments show that penalty goals still outnumber tries in matches between the five more equally-matched sides. In 2021, penalties between the former Five Nations teams totalled fifty, as opposed to forty-three tries scored. In 2022 the forty penalty goals were one more than the total tries scored.

Each of the semi-finals in the 2019 Rugby World Cup were won by the side scoring the most penalty goals and the final saw ten penalties kicked. These figures suggest that there is a lot of life in the penalty goal yet.

Whatever the future holds, the penalty goal has been one

113

of the defining features of rugby union for over a hundred years, long after its original intention had been forgotten – proving once again, that what happened in rugby in the 1880s and 1890s continues to shape the game in the 21st Century.

---

[1] WW Wakefield 'Foreword' in W. Wooller and D. Owen (eds), *Fifty Years of the All Blacks*, (London: 1955) p. 6.
[2] Arthur Guillemard, 'The Past Season' in C.W. Alcock (ed.), *The Football Annual* (London: 1880) p. 58.
[3] Rowland Hill, 'The Past Season' in C.W. Alcock (ed.), *The Football Annual* (London: 1882) p. 21.
[4] RJ Phillips, *The Story of Scottish Rugby* (Edinburgh: 1925) p. 12.

21.

Why Does Hull Have Two Professional Rugby Teams?

Like my father and his father, I am a born and bred supporter of Hull Kingston Rovers, the pride of East Hull. But if it had not been for the strange events of 1895, it would be Hull FC, not KR, who would be the representatives of the east of the city. Rovers would be the pride of West Hull, and I would be a proud supporter of the black and whites.

Hull are the elder of the clubs by a considerable distance. Rugby began in Hull in 1865 when the sons of some of the city's leading business families formed Hull Football Club.

WHH Hutchinson, heir to a family shipbuilding business and the first Yorkshire player to play for the England rugby union side, was educated at Rugby School. His friends the Harrison brothers, of whom Gilbert would also represent England, were educated at Cheltenham College, and Charles Beevor Lambert went to St Peter's School in York. This was the era of twenty-a-side rugby, and so the five sons of the vicar of St Mary's Church in the centre of Hull made up a quarter of the side.

Initially, Hull FC played at the Harrison brothers' family home in North Ferriby but, as rugby clubs sprung up across Yorkshire, the team moved to Selby to make it easier to play opponents from the West Riding. They moved to central Hull in 1871 at the Rifle Volunteer barracks on Londesborough Street, conveniently near Hull's Paragon Station, and today part of the walk from city centre to FC's current stadium. The club could now realistically claim to be Yorkshire's leading rugby club. In 1872, it became the county's first team to join the Rugby Football Union, and two years later was one of five clubs who created what became the Yorkshire Rugby Union.

In 1877, the Yorkshire Cup was started. It was an instant success: when Hull visited Heckmondwike in a cup-tie, the players were astounded at the size of the crowd, as William Hutchinson recalled:

> There was so much excitement over the match among the local public that we really were fortunate in getting away from the ground without having to fight our way out ... the spectators swarmed all about the field and there was a scene that up to that time we had not been accustomed to.[1]

Dozens of rugby clubs were soon created all over Hull. They were often supported by local employers, such as the Hull Dock Company club and Earle's Engineers. Others were based at local pubs, such as Hull Marlborough. Typical of these new clubs was Hull Southcoates, who played in the Courteney Street area in the east of the city. As one old player remembered, the team was 'composed of horny-handed sons of toil.' Southcoates were so successful that they recruited players from as far afield as Wakefield.

Why Does Hull Have Two Professional Rugby Teams?

In 1884, the *Hull Times* began a knock-out competition for local clubs. By 1888, there were 34 in the first round of the cup, from as far afield as Goole, Selby and York. Supporters could also purchase the *Hull Football Almanack*, a guide to the local game with full colour illustrations of the captains of its top teams. The following year saw the start of the *Hull and East Riding Athlete*, a weekly paper devoted to local sports which spent a considerable amount of space reporting on the city's most popular sport.

Hull sides were also enthusiastic participants in Yorkshire-wide tournaments. In 1888, Hull Britannia won the Yorkshire Church Temperance Challenge Shield. The competition had begun the previous year to 'promote an interest in football among the younger churchmen of Yorkshire and, secondly, to keep them out of the public houses.' Clubs with such premises as their headquarters were not allowed to take part – but this didn't stop Britannia from proudly displaying the trophy at their local pub on the victorious return home.

This flouting of the spirit of the temperance competition had a deeper significance than just over-enthusiastic celebrations. The huge influx of working-class players and supporters since the late 1870s had caused rugby in Hull to fracture, just like in the rest of the north of England. Working-class teams could often defeat those who had learnt the game at private schools and universities.

Hull FC were one of those patrician clubs to suffer at the hands of the dockers and factory workers who participated. Its morale had been badly shaken by heavy defeats to local rivals Hull White Star. East Hull's first significant club, White Star were formed in the mid-1870s by cricketers who wished to stay fit during winter. Unlike the elite Hull FC, White Star was more socially open and mixed – its committee included a plumber, commercial traveler, clerk and two pub landlords.

For the elite Hull FC this humiliation by what it saw as social inferiors – and had once even refused to play – was too much to bear. So, in May 1881, Hull FC's annual general meeting decided: 'That this club cease to exist, subject to the White Star club taking our name and admitting our members.' The merged outfit played at Holderness Road, which runs through the heart of East Hull.

The fact that Hull's premier sports club was based there showed how the city itself was changing. In 1885, Alexandra Dock opened as the docks began to expand. Major industrial employers such as Reckitt's and Needler's built factories east of the River Hull. Hull's sporting life focused on the west of the city up until the 1870s, but the rapid growth of east Hull created new communities and rivalries.

Between 1871 and 1901 Hull's population almost doubled from 136,000 people to more than a quarter of a million. For a significant proportion of new citizens rugby was a way to integrate with their neighbours. To cope with increasingly large crowds, Hull installed new grandstands at their ground in 1882 and 1883, and even considered buying the Botanical Gardens on Spring Bank in 1887 to build a bigger stadium.

Larger crowds meant that, until the RFU banned payments in 1886, Hull often paid players to take time off work – aka 'broken time'. Hull's 1884 annual accounts openly listed £18 expenditure on doing just that. The minute book for 1883-84 shows at least three broken time payments for Yorkshire Cup matches, including when the club asked all players not to work on the morning of their first-ever Cup final.[2]

Rugby in Hull, as in the rest of northern England, was now dominated by the working class. This was seen most clearly in the rise of Kingston Amateurs, a club in the Hessle Road docklands area of West Hull. Formed in 1882 by apprentice boilermakers working at two shipbuilding companies, C.D.

Why Does Hull Have Two Professional Rugby Teams?

Holmes, and Amos & Smith, the club changed its name to Kingston Rovers three years later.

In 1888, it won the *Hull Times* Cup for the first time and played at the Hessle Road Locomotive cricket ground at Dairycoates, not too far from what would later become Hull City's Boothferry Park stadium. In February 1892, Rovers' status as Hull's second major rugby club was confirmed when it moved to the newly opened Boulevard (then called the Hull Athletic Ground) midway between Hessle and Anlaby roads, at the heart of Hull's fishing community.

The Athletic Ground, built by a consortium led by the Sheriff of Hull, also staged athletics and cycling tournaments. But only rugby could provide enough spectators to finance the new venue. And it would be the economics of commercial sport that would cause the most sensational change in Hull's sporting geography.

In 1895, Rovers' three-year lease on the ground ran out. It offered to pay the same rent as before, but Hull FC, frustrated at Holderness Road crowd limits, offered the Boulevard's owners three times the rent paid by Rovers, who were soon told to vacate the premises and look for pastures new.

Eventually, they found them in East Hull, on the former ground of Hull Southcoates rugby club at Craven Street. Although the switch from West to East caused a little friction with supporters – although nothing like the rioting in the streets such a move would cause today – Rovers quickly integrated into East Hull and co-opted a number of former Hull Southcoates officials into the club.

Hull FC's mirror-image move from East to West Hull was also highly successful. In their first season back in the west, crowds grew by more than 60 per cent. The club eventually bought the ground in 1899 for £6,500 and officially renamed it the Boulevard.

But the move to West Hull was not the only reason for Hull's increased crowds. Hull were one of the founding members of the Northern Union in August 1895, and that organisation not only brought more spectators to matches but also found deep support among Hull's sporting community.

A letter in the *Hull Daily Mail* a few days after the split probably spoke for the vast majority of rugby fans in the city: 'The clubs who have struck a blow for freedom are to be commended for throwing off the cloak of hypocrisy, conceit and subterfuge, and standing out for those essentially English characteristics – honesty and straight forwardness.'[3]

A fortnight after that, a special meeting of the Hull and District Rugby Union voted 33-24 to resign from the RFU and join the Northern Union, the first of many local rugby organisations to do so. Two years later, after Rovers had won the rugby union double of the Yorkshire Cup and league, they too became a Northern Union club.

As in many other cities across the north of England, the old game of rugby union was eclipsed and for the next decade the new Northern Union reigned supreme across the city, east and west. Hull was now a two-team town, a fact that would define both rugby and the city itself.

---

[1] *Yorkshire Evening Post*, 1 Dec 1900.
[2] A facsimile of the minute book is in the Rugby Football League Archive at Heritage Quay, University of Huddersfield.
[3] *Hull Daily Mail*, 4 Sept 1895.

22.

Is *This Sporting Life* Really A Film About Rugby?

When people discuss the greatest sports film of all time, there are usually two contenders. Martin Scorsese's 1980 *Raging Bull* and Lindsay Anderson's 1963 *This Sporting Life*. But I'm not sure that Anderson's masterpiece is actually about rugby league – or sport – at all.

It was a very important film of the early 1960s. Richard Harris, who played the central character Frank Machin, was nominated for an Oscar and won best actor at that year's Cannes Film Festival. Rachel Roberts, who played Machin's landlady and lover Margaret Hammond, was also nominated for an Oscar and won a BAFTA for best actress.

It is very authentic, shot largely in Leeds and at rugby league grounds at Wakefield Trinity (for the match scenes) and Halifax (for the external, post-match shots). Somewhat incongruously, a library shot of a crowd at Twickenham can be fleetingly glimpsed after Machin scores a try.

It also made full use of Wakefield Trinity's players, and the first words in the film are spoken by Trinity coach and former Great Britain player Ken Traill. One of its most memorable scenes is a flowing movement leading to a try mid-way through the film, actually footage of Wakefield's 5-2 defeat of Wigan in a quarter-final of the 1963 RL Challenge Cup.

The film is a very close adaptation of David Storey's 1960 novel of the same title, not least because Storey wrote the screenplay himself. Much of the original tale was based on its author's own experience. Born into a mining family in Wakefield in 1933, Storey won a scholarship to the local Queen Elizabeth Grammar School.

Upon leaving, he studied at London's Slade School of Fine Art while playing rugby league for Leeds reserve grade 'A' team at the weekends. He'd signed for Leeds at the age of eighteen because, he later recounted, 'what I really wanted to do was go to art school. Taking the Leeds contract was going to be the only way I could pay for my education.'[1]

Storey's life was that of a classic working-class grammar school boy, caught between two contrasting and conflicting worlds. 'Being perceived as an effete art student often made the dressing room a very uncomfortable place for me,' he said. Nor was his time at art school happy: 'At the Slade, meanwhile, I was seen as a bit of an oaf.'[2]

To add to this sense of alienation, when Storey signed for Leeds his grammar school deputy headmaster wrote to tell him he 'had ignominiously let [the school] down.' As he recalled in his posthumously published memoir, *A Stinging Delight*: 'Professionalism and sport in those days were viewed in much the same way as prostitution in relationship to marriage. I'd become, in the view of my former mentors, a whore.'[3]

At the heart of *This Sporting Life* is the relationship between

Is *This Sporting Life* Really A Film About Rugby?

the rugby league player Arthur Machin and his widowed landlady Valerie Hammond (the film changed their names to Frank and Margaret), which combines a finely wrought understanding of the emotional entanglement of the couple with an accurate, if one-sided, description of the seamier realities of rugby league.

Machin is largely impervious to the world around *him*, while Mrs Hammond is crushed by the world around *her*. Both novel and film are part of what was known from the late 1950s as the 'British kitchen sink' drama movement, which aimed, almost for the first time in mainstream British culture, to portray the lives of working-class people in a realistic and sympathetic way. Its most prominent examples were Shelagh Delaney's *A Taste of Honey*, and Alan Sillitoe's *Saturday Night and Sunday Morning* and *The Loneliness of the Long Distance Runner*.

But *This Sporting Life* differs fundamentally from those films because Frank Machin is not a rebel. He does not reject society's norms. His desire is to conform and to be accepted – but he cannot do this because of his inability to understand the rules by which he is expected to live his life.

When the film was released in 1963, it was welcomed by some in rugby league for putting the sport in the public eye. Richard Harris was made an honorary president of Wakefield Trinity whose players and officials were invited to its West End premiere. But many others were not so sure. Hull Kingston Rovers complained that the film was 'detrimental to the rugby league code.' Reviewing it for the weekly *Rugby Leaguer* newspaper, Raymond Fletcher said: 'My worst fears of the film ... were unfortunately realised.'[4]

However, when viewed closely, the film is not actually about rugby league or sport. It is about relationships and the stifling conformity that distorts them and crushes the human spirit. Rugby league is part of the complex social structure that is the backdrop for the personal drama that unfolds. The game's acute sense of class and roots in industrial working-class culture are used by Storey to highlight the underlying emotional tensions of working-class life with a directness that would be impossible using either soccer, where full-time professionalism distanced players from the local community, or rugby union, which was animated by a middle-class value system.

If Tennessee Williams had been born in Castleford, Yorkshire, rather than Columbus, Mississippi, *This Sporting Life* is perhaps a screenplay he would have written. Subtle class hierarchies, suffocating social norms and transgressive and dysfunctional relationships are as central to *This Sporting Life* as they were to plays like *A Streetcar Named Desire*. Indeed, Richard Harris's somewhat uneven performance – he never manages to master a Yorkshire accent – is derived from Marlon Brando's portrayal of Stanley Kowalski in Elia Kazan's 1951 film version of *Streetcar*.

And as with Williams's work, sexuality is central to *This Sporting Life*. In the opening scene, after Machin has his teeth broken by a stiff-arm tackle that leaves him unconscious, the first thing Ken Traill says to him is: 'You won't want to see any tarts for a week.'

Before he signs for the rugby league team, Machin's first encounter with its players is at a dance in the city centre when he cuts in between a young woman and future team-mate. When told to get lost, Machin refuses, and the player says: 'Do you want a thumping, love?'[5] The use of the word 'love' between two men, though in common usage in the Yorkshire coalfields until at least the 1980s, would have appeared to most film-goers to be at odds with the aggressively masculine world portrayed on the screen.

Is *This Sporting Life* Really A Film About Rugby?

What makes the film most interesting, perhaps, is almost all of its relationships fall outside of the boundaries of what would be assumed to be normal or respectable in 1950s Britain. The main one is between Machin and the widow with whom he lodges, Mrs Hammond. Her husband was killed in an industrial accident in a factory owned by club chairman, Gerald Weaver, leaving her with two small children. The relationship between Machin and Mrs Hammond is cold and almost entirely uncomfortable, even when he falls in love with her. It culminates in him violently raping her.

Mrs Hammond is also significantly older than Machin. Her life experience, much of it tragic, is something much younger Frank does not understand. Their age difference clearly falls outside of what is deemed to be a 'respectable' relationship, as seen by the reactions of Mrs Hammond's neighbours to Frank, especially when he gives her a fur coat, much to the silent disgust of her visiting friend.

Machin's other major relationship is with club scout 'Dad' Johnson, who Mrs Hammond suspects is attracted to Frank: 'He ogles you. He looks at you like a girl', she complains. Johnson's effeminacy, as portrayed by William Hartnell, is continually emphasised by Mrs Hammond, who complains he has soft hands, and also in a scene when the players pass a ball to Johnson, who drops it – a sure sign of unmanliness in this intensely competitive male world.

Gerald Weaver's interest in Frank also appears to be about more than rugby. Wonderfully played by Alan Badel, he gives Machin a lift home in his car, and ostentatiously puts his hand on Frank's knee, an act Frank clearly suspects is something more than mere friendliness.

Machin's other transgressive relationship is with Weaver's wife (played by Vanda Godsell), who attempts to seduce him. Frank is clearly not the first player Mrs Weaver has invited back home. Arthur Lowe's character, club director Charles Slomer, warns Frank about what he calls 'Mrs Weaver's weakness for social informalities.'

All of which highlights how *This Sporting Life* presents a range and complexity of relationships in ways previously unseen in British film. This was because Storey and Lindsay Anderson, consciously or otherwise, set the film's shifting relationships against the norms of sport. Anderson, the public-school educated gay intellectual, is the outsider looking in, while Storey, the working-class rugby league-playing grammar school boy, is the insider looking out.

Both understood that sport was a masculine, heterosexual world, in which might is right and weakness punished, a world Frank Machin understands. But Machin's mastery of that world puts him at a disadvantage amid the real and complex realities of sex and personal relationships. That tension is the driving force of the film.

To some extent *This Sporting Life* presents an unfairly brutal and bleak portrait of rugby league; it is noticeable that no player expresses any enjoyment in playing the game. But the sport is only a vehicle for the film to present the complexity of human relationships against the oppressive conformity of gender roles and class distinction.

The portrayal of sport is rarely successful in films – but *This Sporting Life* is very successful, largely because it is not really about sport – or rugby league – at all.

It's about sex.

---

[1] *Observer Sports Monthly*, 8 May 2005.
[2] *The Guardian*, 31 Jan 2005.
[3] David Storey, *A Stinging Delight* (London: 2021) p. 80.
[4] *Rugby Leaguer*, 15 Feb 1963.
[5] All quotes are from the film rather than the book.

23.

When Rugby League Was Almost A Jewish Game...

For a long time rugby league has prided itself on inclusivity, especially when compared to other sports. Most notably, black players have taken the field in international rugby league regularly from the 1930s.

But they weren't the only minority group to find a home in the sport. It is often not realised that people from the Jewish community have played a significant role in rugby league, on and off the field, from its very beginnings.

In fact, it is important to realise that Jews have made a major contribution to the history of modern sport in general, ever since it emerged in the 1700s.

To take one example, arguably the most famous British boxer of the late 1700s was London's Daniel Mendoza, who came from a Sephardic Jewish family and was English boxing champion between 1792 and 1795. He was one of numerous Jewish prizefighters active between 1760 and 1820, the most notable among them being Samuel Elias, Aby Belasco, Barney Aaron and Elisha Crabbe.

Almost a century later, in 1889, another Jewish boxer, Alf Bowman, won the British amateur heavyweight title and, two years after that, Edward Levy won the British amateur weightlifting championship. Perhaps the most prominent Jewish sports official of that era was Montague Shearman, secretary of the Amateur Athletic Association and author of one of the earliest histories of the football codes, 1887's *Athletics and Football*.

The Jewish community's relationship with rugby in the north of England began at a similar time. From the early 1880s, tens of thousands of Jewish people fled from anti-Semitism in Tsarist Russia and settled in Britain. Many boarded ships that docked in Hull and from there they moved on to the major cities of the north, especially Leeds and Manchester. The Jewish population of Britain grew quickly, from 60,000 in 1882 to a quarter of a million by 1914.

They settled in working-class city areas such as Broughton in Manchester – home of rugby league's first league and cup double winners Broughton Rangers – and the Leylands, in the centre of Leeds. A short walk from the Leylands was the home ground of Leeds Parish Church rugby club, then one of the most successful teams in the city.

The rugby club had been started in 1874 by the church (today known as Leeds Minster) as a way to spread the Christian gospel there, but the great rugby boom of the 1880s transformed them into one of the top sides in the north, and the club reached the quarter-finals of the Challenge Cup in 1900.

By that time, however, a large proportion of its fans were Jewish. It was their local club and like many other working-class people in Leeds, the game captured their hearts, despite

When Rugby League Was Almost A Jewish Game

matches being played on the Sabbath, Saturday. Indeed, probably to the annoyance of the church, the club became known throughout Leeds as the 'Jewish team'. Whether this was a contributory factor to the church closing the club down in 1901 isn't known, but it probably didn't help.

Jewish players began to emerge at this time too. Eli Jacobson debuted for Leeds Parish Church in September 1892 and also played for Leeds, Holbeck (before they became Leeds United) and Hunslet, then the leading team in the area. He also played 12 times for Yorkshire and, in 1897, was presented with a special commemorative medal by the Leeds Jewish community for his athletic achievements.

Jacobson was a local butcher and once his playing career was over, he became involved in the Leeds amateur rugby league scene. In 1929, he donated a cup to be played for every year by factories in Hunslet. Open to all teams within eight miles of Hunslet, the Eli Jacobson Cup attracted 36 teams in its second year and continued until the Second World War. Sadly Eli died in October 1932 in a bizarre accident, when he slipped on a cabbage leaf at work and died of his injuries.

Although an important figure on and off the rugby fields of Leeds, Eli wasn't the biggest Jewish star in the game. The biggest names in the 1890s were brothers Evan and David James, star Swansea half-backs and sons of a Jewish mother from Cornwall. They were capped for Wales in 1890 and then controversially moved to Broughton Rangers in 1892. They were temporarily banned from rugby union, but eventually went back to Swansea before returning to play rugby league in 1899. They were followed in the 1900s by local Broughton boy Reuben Glaskie who starred for Rangers.

But far and away the most important Jewish player of rugby league's first 25 years was Albert Rosenfeld.

The son of a tailor in Sydney, Rosenfeld was born in 1885

and signed for Eastern Suburbs as a teenager. He was one of the pioneers of Australian rugby league, playing for Australia in the first-ever match against Albert Baskerville's All Golds in 1907. He was an automatic choice for the first Kangaroo touring team to Britain in 1908.

While on tour, he caught the eye of Huddersfield and came back to play on the wing for the club in 1909. Under the leadership of Harold Wagstaff, the side became known as the team of all talents, and Rosenfeld was one of its greatest. He was a prodigious try-scorer. In the 1911-12 season he scored an unbelievable 78 tries. This appeared to be a record never to be broken – but two years later Rosenfeld eclipsed his own feat with an amazing 80 tries in the campaign. He ended his career with 389 tries in 388 matches, standing alongside Brian Bevan and Billy Boston as one of the very few players who averaged more than a try a match in their career.

The 1920s and 1930s saw a number of Jewish players follow in Rosenfeld's footsteps, such as Hull KR captain Louis Harris, Rochdale's Sam Birkinshaw and a number of Broughton Rangers players. Rangers' Lester Samuels, one of the few qualified doctors to play rugby league, operated as an amateur because that allowed him to play on Saturday. Had he played for money on the Sabbath it would make it work and therefore forbidden.

Broughton also had significant Jewish representation among club directors and officials. Barney Manson, born into the Manchester Jewish community but a director of Swinton, became a manager of the 1958 Great Britain touring team. Louis Harris became a director of Hull KR, and was followed by his nephew Max Gold in the 1970s, who became club chairman and oversaw the club's move from its old Craven Park ground in 1989.

During the inter-war years, rugby league was deeply

When Rugby League Was Almost A Jewish Game

embedded in the Jewish communities of Leeds, Hull and Manchester. Leeds Judeans played an annual match against Hull Judeans in the 1920s. Many schools in Jewish areas had teams and sides from Jewish-owned factories were a common sight in workshop competitions. Some older Leeds fans could recall that Yiddish songs were sometimes sung on the Headingley terraces during the 1930s.

The number of top-flight Jewish rugby league players was never large, but it was still significantly more than the four Jewish players whom the *Jewish Chronicle* recorded in 1935 as ever having played in the Football League.[1] Nevertheless, it was another small indication of league's willingness to recruit on the basis of merit rather than social or racial status.

Sadly, that does not mean the game was free of anti-Semitism. 'But we don't bring supporters from Jerusalem,' was the alleged response of a St Helens supporter in 1929 when Salford fans criticised the number of New Zealanders in the Saints' team, and anti-Semitic comments against Leeds could occasionally be heard at matches.

The popularity of rugby league in the Jewish community during the 1930s was sometimes bemoaned by a number of more orthodox Jews. The famous mathematician and Zionist leader Selig Brodetsky, who lived in Leeds, complained about the number of Jews he saw going to watch rugby at Headingley on the Sabbath.[2]

The north of England was not the only place where Jews found a sporting home in rugby league. In Sydney in 1924 the Lieberman Cup, which billed itself as the 'Jewish RL competition', started with four teams: the Maccabean Sports and Athletic Club, Judean Social Sports Club, the Young Persons Hebrew Association, and the Maccabi Institute, for whom Lionel van Praag, 1936 World Speedway Champion, played. The league lasted until 1927 but even after it ended the Sydney newspaper *Hebrew Standard* could say: 'As a winter pastime Rugby League is regarded by red-blooded young men as second to none.'[3]

After World War Two, Jewish participation on the field declined. But this was not just the case for rugby league. As the Jewish community became more prosperous, the use of sport to find a way out of poverty also declined. In Britain the number of Jewish boxers – a sport they dominated in the 1930s – fell away and, in America, Jewish participation in basketball, another game once thought of as a 'Jewish sport', also declined massively.

The last great Jewish rugby league player was South African Springbok winger Wilf Rosenberg, who played for Leeds and Hull from 1959 to 1963, scoring over a hundred tries in fewer than 170 matches. Probably the last Jewish professional player in Britain was Castleford and Bramley's Darren Coen in the 1980s, while in Australia it appears that Souths' forward Ian Rubin was the last player of Jewish heritage to play in the NRL.

Yet despite all the changes society has undergone over the past century, a Jewish presence remains. Between 2016 and 2020 Todd Greenberg was the chief executive of the NRL and in 2019 Simon Johnson was appointed chairman of the RFL.

In his great book, *The Joy of Yiddish*, Leo Rosten makes the point that Yiddish, the language of European Ashkenazi Jews, was never the language of a ruling class.

And in a similar way, rugby league, wherever it has been played, has never been the sport of a ruling class either.

---

[1] *Jewish Chronicle*, 15 March 1935.
[2] Selig Brodetsky, *The Intellectual Level of Anglo-Jewish Life* (London: 1928) p.6.
[3] Anthony Hughes, 'Muscular Judaism and the Jewish Rugby League Competition in Sydney, 1924-1927', *Sporting Traditions* (1996) 13:1, p. 66.

24.

How Lucius Banks Became America's First Pro Rugby Player And Rugby's First Black Pro

Who was the first American to play professional rugby?
Who was the first transatlantic rugby league player?
Who was the first black athlete to play professional rugby league?

The answer is exactly the same for all three questions.

Lucius Banks.

Anyone who has dug around in the early history of rugby league may have come across a man who, in January 1912, made his debut on the left wing for Hunslet against York. But little else is known about the remarkable life he led and, sadly, his pioneering feats have largely been forgotten.

Banks was born in 1888 in Harmony Village, Virginia, some sixty miles from Richmond, the city that was the capital of the slave-owning Confederacy during the American Civil War. The war had ended only twenty-three years earlier, so it's probable that his parents were born into slavery. While their boy was very young, the family moved to Arlington, Massachusetts, a small, predominantly white town six miles from Boston, where his father found work as a manual labourer.

Young Lucius attended Arlington High, where, despite being one of only a few black students in a deeply segregated part of America, he was the starting pitcher for its baseball team and also wrote for the school magazine. On graduation, he joined the US Army's 9th Cavalry Regiment.

The 9th was what was then known as 'a coloured unit', which meant that, in line with the racial segregation imposed in the US Army at that time, it comprised entirely African-American soldiers. Lucius seems to have been part of its 100-man detachment based at the US Military Academy at West Point in New York State. The 9th Cavalrymen were there to teach elite, white, cadets the art of horse-riding and Banks was one of those teachers.

While there, he played for the Cavalry regiment's baseball and American football sides and, while playing quarterback in a football match in 1911, he was spotted by a member of Hunslet's rugby league committee, on business in New York. It's unclear who it was or what his business was in America.

Nevertheless, on 10 July 1911 the Hunslet committee discussed a report about Lucius Banks and decided to offer him a contract to move to Yorkshire. As Banks was in the Army, he told Hunslet he would need the consent of his commanding officer so, that September, the club wrote to Captain G.V. Henry explaining the position. Henry appears to have raised no objections to the pioneering move, and history was about to be made.

Lucius Banks was not rugby league's first black player. A 1903 photo of the Pendlebury amateur team has an unnamed black player in its line-up. But he was the first recorded black

How Lucius Banks Became America's First Pro Rugby Player

professional. He was followed in 1913 by Jimmy Peters, who signed for Barrow after an illustrious rugby union career with Bristol, Plymouth, and England.

By signing for Hunslet, Banks also became one of the first African-Americans to be a professional player of any code of football. In American football, the first black professional was Charles Follis, who in 1904 signed a contract with the Shelby Blues of the short-lived Ohio League. But this was long before the NFL, and pro-football at that time was a series of badly organised short-lived regional leagues that had no national presence. So Lucius Banks was the first black American professional to play in a nationally-organised football league.

He made his rugby league debut on 17 January 1912 when, in that game against York, he scored a try in front of 6,000 people at Hunslet's Parkside. He scored tries in his next four matches too, no doubt helped by the fact that his centre partner was the immortal Billy Batten. It also seems that the club thought his experience at quarterback would translate to stand-off, so he began the next season as a number six.

This was not so far-fetched as it might appear. The forward pass had only been legalised in American football in 1906 and was not yet widely used, so a quarterback's role was to hand-off, laterally pass or run himself. Hunslet were committed to his long-term success, clearly: 'The lad will feel a little strange for a short time [and] we hope that he will receive every encouragement,' read the club programme. To help him settle in, the committee found him a job with a local saddler.[1]

However, despite the fact that there is no indication the Hunslet committee ever gave a thought to the colour of their new signing's skin (the programme, for example, does not seem to have mentioned it) the local press sought to whip up racism. A letter protesting the 'importation of a foreigner' that didn't mention colour was disgustingly headlined 'Hunslet's

Coloured Coon' by the *Yorkshire Evening Post*, while the *Yorkshire Post* complained about the 'gimmick' of 'coloured players from America.'[2] Hunslet were outraged and in March 1912 demanded a public apology from the newspapers, 'with the same publicity' as had been given to the original insults.[3]

Despite the racism of the local press, Lucius seems to have been popular with fans and made a real contribution to the team. In November 1912, he was even compared to Batten when he leapt over a Bradford tackler, a skill now confined to the gridiron code. This was also a time of change for Hunslet. The great team led by Albert Goldthorpe that had done the grand slam of All Four Cups in 1908 was breaking up, club uncertain about how to recapture its glory years.

In December 1912, Lucius opted to return to the USA. He had not successfully made the transition from quarterback to stand-off and, probably more importantly, the contrast between living in New York state and south Leeds may have resulted in significant homesickness. On Boxing Day 1912, Hunslet's programme announced that he would be returning home on New Year's Eve: 'We know you all will join with us in wishing him a pleasant voyage and every success in the future.'[4]

And there, it appears, the sporting career of a man who had been the first American professional rugby player, the first transatlantic league player, and the first black athlete to play top-flight rugby league, ended.

He returned home to the Boston area and, when America entered the First World War in 1917, joined the 349th Field Artillery, with whom he served in France as a first lieutenant. War over, he joined the Boston Police Dept. In September 1919, Boston policemen had gone on strike and the governor of Massachusetts, future US president Calvin Coolidge, refused to negotiate and recruited new cops to replace the

How Lucius Banks Became America's First Pro Rugby Player

strikers. Banks was one such recruit, joining up in November 1919. He soon found racism was as rife in the police service as it was elsewhere in the United States.

In the summer of 1922, he arrested a drunken white man who had propositioned two black women in the street. However, the man complained he had been roughly treated and when his case came to trial was acquitted. The accused had powerful friends – one of his character witnesses was local state senator George Curran – and it appears that Banks became a marked man. In 1926, he was dismissed from the police for unspecified 'conduct unbecoming an officer.'

His dismissal became an important campaign for the city's black community. In 1932, the Massachusetts state house of representatives overwhelmingly voted for his reinstatement into the police. One representative stated openly that Lucius Banks had been 'framed out of the police department because he is a coloured man.' He was reinstated, but it wasn't until May 1950, fully eighteen years later, that he finally received financial compensation, and this was only because the state's house of representatives passed an act authorising payment of seven and a half thousand dollars. But by this time he had been retired from the police for six years.

Lucius Banks died in February 1955 and was buried in Arlington cemetery. Such was his standing in the community that the flags on local public buildings flew at half-mast. His son, Richard L. Banks, became Boston's most prominent civil rights lawyer, appointed a judge in 1980. And so the spirit that had taken Lucius Banks to Hunslet lived on.

---

[1] *Parkside Echo*, match programme 27 Jan 1912.
[2] *Yorkshire Evening Post* and *Yorkshire Post*, both 26 Jan 1912.
[3] Hunslet club committee minutes, 19 March 1912.
[4] *Parkside Echo*, 26 Dec 1912.

25.

Did Melrose Invent Rugby Sevens? It's Complicated...

Seven-a-side rugby used to be something played for fun once the serious business of the season had ended. But what was a relaxing way to ease into the off-season is now big business in rugby union. Rugby Sevens is an Olympic sport and the Sevens circuit tours the world, almost a parallel universe of corporate hospitality and instant try-scoring gratification.

The new found popularity of 'limited player' rugby has been inspired partially by the success of Twenty-20 cricket. Sports administrators tend to be herd animals, so if one sport discovers a successful formula it doesn't take long for a bandwagon to start rolling. Even Aussie Rules tried to get in on the act in 2018 with its shortlived seven-a-side AFL-X.

None have been as commercially successful as T-20, but rugby has a far longer history of limited player innovations going back almost 140 years.

If you read any histories of Sevens rugby union you will

Did Melrose Invent Rugby Sevens? It's Complicated...

have been told that it was invented in Melrose, in Scotland's Border Region, in 1883. But, as is usual in rugby history, this isn't quite the full story.

Rugby in Scotland emerged in the elite private schools of Edinburgh in the 1850s and 1860s. But in the 1870s it became popular in the small industrial towns of the Borders, where woollen cloth was the most important product. Galashiels specialised in tweed, Melrose in linen and Hawick in hosiery and knitwear. The rivalry between these towns helped to fuel the emergence of clubs. Hawick rugby club was formed in 1873, followed by Gala in 1875, Kelso the following year, and Melrose the year after that.

Rugby in the Borders was passionate and intense, a game which brought together the local businessman and the factory worker, just as it did in Northern England and South Wales.

Scottish Border towns had much in common with their fellow rugby-playing textile towns in England, not least an enthusiasm for summer sports festivals where the best local talent was on show, and often rewarded. This popular culture was almost a world away from the elite amateur atmosphere of Edinburgh's patrician rugby clubs, two worlds that rarely met. No player from the Borders was selected for Scotland before Galashiel's Adam Dalgleish made his debut in the Scottish pack against Wales in 1890, almost twenty years after the Scots' first international match.

One major difference between the clubs in Edinburgh and the Borders was the region's love of seven-a-side rugby. The first such tournament was staged by Melrose on 28 April 1883, part of a range of attractions at the Melrose Sports Carnival. Its appeal was sealed when Melrose defeated its deadly rival Gala in the final. Now the flame of local rivalry had been lit, the event became an annual affair. And so, according to the rugby history books, limited-player rugby was born.

The idea was apparently suggested by a local butcher and player, Ned Haig, as a way to raise funds for the club. It's possible he was inspired by the small-sided games of soccer that had taken place at Scottish athletics festivals since at least 1880, when Glasgow Rangers were defeated in the final of the six-a-side tournament by the home side at Alexandra Athletic Club's annual sports carnival.[1]

But the Melrose competition was not the first time a small-sided version of rugby had been played. In September 1879, the first recorded example of limited player rugby was staged when the Huddersfield Cricket & Athletic Club (today's Huddersfield Giants) hosted a six-a-side tournament. As well as Huddersfield, Leeds, Dewsbury, Bradford, Leeds St John's (now Leeds Rhinos), Bradford Juniors and Kirkstall entered for the chance to win six small silver cups, with six leather bags for the runners-up. Playing regular rugby rules in ten-minute halves, Huddersfield's six overran Leeds 23-0 in the final.[2]

Over the next three or four years, Dewsbury, Bramley, Cleckheaton, Wakefield and Leeds Parish Church all staged similar contests. Six-a-side competitons were played during the summer, usually at athletics carnivals, with the aim of raising money for the club or, more often, hospital charities. But by the mid-1880s the popularity of six-a-sides had been eclipsed by nine-a-side rugby.

In August 1881, Batley staged the first nine-a-side tournament. Seven clubs entered, competing for a first prize of nine Vienna Regulators, a type of pendulum wall clock valued at £2 10s each. Runners-up received a gentleman's travelling bag each. It was not accidental that the value of prizes was always publicised, ensuring players understood that they were playing for something a little bit more tangible than simple glory.

Did Melrose Invent Rugby Sevens? It's Complicated...

Batley were defeated by their neighbours Dewsbury in the final, but a close match ended in uproar as players argued with the referee about which side had won, as described by the Batley historian C.F. Shaw:

...when the referee, a Mr Bentley of Heckmondwike, was appealed to, he waived his decision which so exasperated a certain section of the crowd that a free fight ensued. The referee was expected to attend a meeting of the Batley committee, but failed to make his appearance, as he had received several threatening letters in regard to the contest; and the committee decided to submit the matter to the editor of the *Athletic News*, and abide by his decision, which was given in favour of Dewsbury.[3]

Batley made itself the centre of summer nine-a-side rugby. In 1885, three thousand people stood outside Batley Town Hall to see the club receive the silver trophy from the mayor. Their opponents in the final were Barrow, who travelled over one hundred miles to be there, demonstrating the wide appeal of the small-sided game to fans and clubs alike. Nine-a-side tournaments were staged throughout the 1880s in Leeds, Castleford, Dewsbury, Huddersfield and also in Lancashire, attracting large crowds and raising thousands of pounds for local charities.

So why did small-sided rugby die out in Northern England? As you might have guessed, the leadership of the Rugby Football Union were not keen on these contests.

Most tournaments were played outside the regular season using modified rules, which the RFU saw as undermining its control of the game. For example, the 1881 Batley tournament was played under its own point-scoring system. A converted try was worth eight points, a goal six and an unconverted try four. But at this time, official rugby union rules only counted goals as a method of scoring.

The second problem for rugby's leaders was that these tournaments were suspected of promoting professionalism. The prizes that could be won were often valuable and it was well-known that players could simply sell the clocks and medals for their cash value. Some tournaments even offered cash prizes, strictly against RFU rules. Wakefield's 1882 six-a-side contest saw the winning Thornes players pick up two pounds each.

In August 1890, the Yorkshire Rugby Union suspended eight teams who had played in a summer six-a-side tournament. The following month, the Lancashire Rugby Union banned all matches played with less than fifteen players per side. Their spokesman told the newspapers that feelings ran 'very strongly against the nine-a-side game during the closed season and it was decided that in future no more contests be allowed during the summer.'[4] This marked the end of the line for small-sided rugby in England, an early victim of the convulsions in rugby that led to the 1895 split.

But in Scotland, the two worlds of Scottish rugby lived in separate spheres which rarely connected. Borders rugby presented no threat to the patrician leadership of the game and seven-a-side rugby was allowed to continue unhindered. And, thanks to judicious historical editing, the 'short game', as it became known in union, was eventually incorporated into mainstream rugby, most notably with the start of the Middlesex Sevens in 1926, organised by the exiled Scot Dr JA Russell-Cargill.

Yet, despite their popularity with crowds, sevens and nines versions never really occupied the same position in rugby league culture as sevens did in rugby union. Sevens became very important to union because it moved away from the set-

Did Melrose Invent Rugby Sevens? It's Complicated...

pieces and goal-kicking of fifteen-a-side rugby and shifted the emphasis to running with the ball, passing and scoring tries. But of course these were the same principles on which rugby league based its own philosophy of the game.

So while rugby union needed sevens as a reminder that there was a different way to play rugby, rugby league had already become that different game.

---

[1] *Glasgow Herald*, 3 May 1880.
[2] *Leeds Mercury*, 16 Sept 1879.
[3] C.F. Shaw, *The Gallant Youths* (Batley: 1899) p. 20.
[4] *Leeds Mercury*, 17 Sept 1890.

26.

How Romanian Rugby Became A Cold War Football

You may have heard of 'Ping Pong Diplomacy', when table tennis was used to develop diplomatic links between Richard Nixon's America and Mao Zedong's China. But this wasn't the first time sport had been used in the East-West Cold War.

In the 1950s and 1960s, the British government used 'Rugger Diplomacy' to promote its interests in Romania, where rugby union became an issue for the British Foreign Office.

Rugby union has a long history in Romania. As a nation, it has deep cultural ties to France. Children of the Romanian elite were often sent to Paris for their education. Bucharest, the capital of Romania, was known as 'Little Paris' and its architecture owed much to the design of the French capital.

In 1913, Romanian students returning home to Bucharest from French universities set up the first rugby clubs. These were Stadiul Roman, modelled on Stade Français, at that time the leading rugby club in France, and Tennis Club Roman,

How Romanian Rugby Became A Cold War Football

which won the first championship in 1914. Two years later, Gregore Caracostea, who had played in Paris for Racing Club de France while a student, set up the Central Commission for Rugby Football, the forerunner of the Romanian Rugby Federation, to administer the sport.

After World War One, Romania played in the 1919 Inter-Allied Games in Paris but lost 48-5 to France and 23-0 to the USA. In 1924, they joined France and USA in the Paris Olympics rugby competition, losing 31-0 to the Americans and 61-3 to France. Even so, they still won the bronze medal because only those three teams competed.

The interwar years were lean times for Romanian rugby. The national side's only wins were against Czechoslovakia in 1927 and the Netherlands in 1937. They finished fourth behind France, Germany and Italy in the May 1936 European Championship in Berlin, which are often referred to as an unofficial Olympic tournament.

Romania were members of the 'Fédération Internationale de Rugby Amateur', set up by the French Rugby Union in January 1934 after its own expulsion from the Five Nations. Alongside France, its two leading nations were Germany and Italy, two countries then under fascist dictatorships, and Romania also became a dictatorship in 1938.

The devastation of World War Two and start of the Cold War meant Romania, now led by the Communist Party and allied with the Soviet Union, didn't restart internationals until 1951, when they beat Czechoslovakia and East Germany.

Rugby union grew in importance tremendously during the 1950s. A number of Communist Party leaders were keen supporters. Manea Mănescu, the Minister of Finance who would become Prime Minister in the 1970s, played the game, and the Minister of Foreign Affairs, Grigore Preoteasa, was also an ex-player and the president of the Romanian Rugby

Federation. These high-level connections meant that rugby was seen by the Romanians as a way to develop contacts with the West. The relationship between Romania and the Soviet Union was not always smooth and the Romanian government sought a more independent foreign policy, so rugby offered new opportunities to open doors.

For its part, as early as 1944 the Foreign Office had identified sport – with 'music, ballet, drama and the like' – as a way of exerting influence to protect British financial interests in the Romanian oil industry. This had become even more important in the 1950s, after the Romanian government nationalised the oil industry. The Foreign Office demanded payment of around one million pounds in compensation for dispossessed British share-holders and payment of what they claimed were outstanding oil royalties.

The dispute became a rugby issue when Swansea undertook a two-game tour of Romania in August 1954. Led by Clem Thomas, the Welshmen lost the first match, 23-12, to Locomotive, a match played in one hundred degree heat, but won the next match against Constructor, 16-5. It is interesting to note that Carwyn James, the future coach of Wales, guested for Swansea on the tour, probably because he spoke Russian.

The tour was organised by Rowe Harding, the former Welsh captain who was now a high court judge and very well connected in Whitehall and the Foreign Office. He also had contacts with the Anglo-Romanian Friendship Society. As anyone who has ever seen a play by David Hare will understand, Harding's informal networks and personal authority were typical of the ways in which the British conducted so-called 'back channel' aspects of foreign policy.

Swansea's tour was so successful in sporting and diplomatic terms that Romania's national team was invited to tour England and Wales in September 1955. The tourists

How Romanian Rugby Became A Cold War Football

stunned British sport by beating Swansea, 19-3, drawing with Harlequins nine-all, and narrowly losing to Cardiff 6-3.

The Romanian tour's success sent shockwaves through British sport. After the success of the Soviet Union and its allies at the 1954 Olympic Games, many people worried that Soviet-bloc sport would soon eclipse the capitalist West. Rowe Harding spoke for many in saying the British should 'emulate the will to win, and copy the training methods which make the communists such formidable opponents'.

The following year, Harlequins visited Bucharest, where they too were defeated, 14-0. This match was a significant diplomatic event, and the touring party was led by the England Grand Slam winning captain of the 1920s and former RFU president, William Wavell Wakefield. Wakefield was not merely one the most authoritative figures in rugby union, he was also a Conservative MP. He would later become chair of the Anglo-Romanian Parliamentary Group.

In 1956, Wakefield returned to Romania and met with Grigore Preoteasa, the Romanian rugby union president who was also the Minister of Foreign Affairs. The Romanians were keen to develop trade links and Wakefield suggested that a rugby tour of Britain would offer an opportunity for informal talks with government officials.

The Romanians returned to play Bristol, Leicester and Gloucester in September 1956. However, behind the scenes the Foreign Office was unhappy with Wakefield, who they considered unreliable. More importantly, they wanted to get the Romanians to make a commitment to compensate oil companies before they agreed to official diplomatic relations.[1]

There was another problem too. On the 1955 tour of Britain one of the Romanian players, Stanislav Luric, told the *Daily Mail* that the players were paid £100 for beating Swansea and £50 for drawing with Harlequins.[2] This confirmed widespread fears that, despite claiming to be amateurs, Soviet-bloc athletes were in reality professionals.

The RFU and International Rugby Board discussed the issue but, as usual, turned a blind eye. In June 1956 Wakefield even told the RFU, without a hint of irony, that 'all sport in Romania is run on amateur lines and no players were paid.'

But behind the scenes, others were not so convinced.

In late 1955, a Foreign Office official told Rowe Harding he had evidence Romanian players were being paid to play, in violation of union's amateur rules. Harding wrote back to the Foreign Office explaining with Machiavellian hypocrisy that: 'It will be difficult now to pull down the iron curtain so far as rugby is concerned. If we amateurs do it, I have no doubt that Romania will turn to rugby league, which will be a tragedy.'[3]

As Harding may have been aware, the Romanians had indeed been investigating rugby league. The secretary of the Romanian Federation had written to the RFL in December 1954, just a few months after Swansea's first visit, asking for more information and to be sent rugby league rule books. Nothing happened, possibly because of the governmental links the union matches had opened up for Romanians, and also perhaps because Bill Fallowfield, the RFL secretary, showed no appetite to pursue the opportunity.[4]

The Foreign Office may also have been trying to undermine Wakefield's attempt to insert himself into their negotiations. The Foreign Office was increasingly frustrated by the Romanians' refusal to compensate shareholders in the British oil companies they had nationalised. So, in August 1956, informal talks were ended because, as a Foreign Office memo explained: 'The Romanians mainly wanted to sell us oil and the oil companies would not buy it without some agreement about compensation for nationalisation.'[5]

Rugby relations between the countries therefore came to

How Romanian Rugby Became A Cold War Football

an end; the September 1956 tour was the last time matches were played until another diplomatic thaw in 1964 when, according to the RFU, the Foreign Office 'intimated' that it would approve of a Harlequins tour of Romania.[6]

If the suspension of British contacts was a political decision so too was the desire of French union to step into the rugby vacuum Britain had created. In 1959, the French government signed a cultural agreement with Romania, opening the way to regular international matches between the two nations.

In home and away matches with France every season, the Romanians showed the same form they had against England and Wales. In May 1960, they beat France 11-5 and in 1961 drew, 5-5, in France. These matches helped turn Romania into Europe's strongest side outside the Five Nations. In contrast, England didn't invite them to play at Twickenham until 1985.

So, despite the RFU claiming sport and politics didn't mix, especially in apartheid South Africa, this example of 'Rugger Diplomacy' showed it was perfectly happy to be part of the Foreign Office's diplomatic strategy towards Romania.

British rugby union opened relations when government policy required it and closed them down when the political winds blew in a different direction.

Once again rugby demonstrated that those who say keep politics out of sport really mean: keep out of sport the politics with which I disagree.

---

[1] Confidential Report from British Legation in Bucharest, 17 May 1956, TNA FO 371/122750.
[2] *Daily Mail*, 8 January 1956.
[3] Harding to Ward, 30 January 1956, TNA FO 371/122750.
[4] I Denicky to W Fallowfield, 8 December 1954. RFL Archives, University of Huddersfield.
[5] Quoted in Mihaela Sitariu, *British-Romanian Relations during the Cold War* (Western University PhD thesis: 2014) p. 125.
[6] RFU Overseas Liaison Committee, 3 Jan 1964.

27.

How Wigan v Bath Showed How Rugby Had Changed... Or Did It?

In 1996, the unthinkable happened. Bath, the dominant team in English rugby union over the previous decade, having just won the league and cup double, played Wigan, the reigning rugby league champions and one of the most successful sides the game had ever seen.

The matches – the first under league rules, the second under union's – were possible because in August 1995 rugby union abandoned 109 years of amateurism, embraced professionalism, and lifted its ban on rugby league.

In one sense, the games were not that interesting. Wigan won the league match, 82-6, and Bath won the union game, 44-19. But the way they are remembered shows us how little has actually changed between rugby's two codes.

This wasn't the first time that union and league teams had played each other. In January 1943, a Northern Command Army league team beat the Northern Command union side,

How Wigan v Bath Showed How Rugby Had Changed...

18-11, under union rules at Headingley. One year later, the Combined Services rugby league team took down a Combined Services union side, 15-10, in a match at Bradford's Odsal stadium that again used union rules. In between, a league side also won the Northern Command's seven-a-side rugby union tournament in May 1943, defeating a union side containing seven internationals in the final.

Although the RFU had temporarily suspended its lifetime ban on league players during World War Two, there was never any question the Army sides would play under league rules. Indeed, any discussion by a union club about playing league from 1895 and 1995 would have meant expulsion from the sport with every player banned from union for life.

So it was inevitable when union went professional that there would be pressure for the top teams in each code to test themselves against each other. Since 1989, Bath had won the championship and Pilkington Cup six times each, doing the double on four occasions. Over the same period, Wigan had been even more dominant, winning the championship and Challenge Cup seven times, and doing the double six times. No team had so dominated either sport before or since.

When the two sides ran out at Maine Road, Manchester, for the rugby league match on 8 May 1996, no-one knew quite what to expect. The previous weekend Bath had completed their fourth double with a narrow win over Leicester in the Pilkington Cup final, so had not had the best preparation. For Wigan, the new summer rugby league season had just started. But ninety seconds after kick-off, when Martin Offiah scored the first of Wigan's sixteen tries, everyone knew precisely what was going to happen. Wigan simply ran Bath ragged with their speed of movement, handling skills and positional sense in attack and defence. When the referee blew his whistle for the end of the first half it was 52-0.

In the Wigan dressing room, Joe Lydon, Wigan's manager, told the team to take their foot off the gas so as not to embarrass Bath and make things difficult for themselves in the return match. Shaun Edwards strongly disagreed and argued they should aim for 100 points. As it was, they slowed the tempo in the second half and at one point played with only eleven men on the pitch. Bath, now playing with unlimited substitutions, got a little more into the game, not least due to Mike Catt's skills at stand-off, and Jon Callard scored a try. But Wigan still scored 30 more points to win 82 points to six. It could have been even worse; under union's points system, the score would have been 98-7.

Little more than two weeks later, on 25 May, the return match under union rules was at Twickenham. In between, Wigan became the first league team to play in the Middlesex Sevens, when they came from behind to beat Wasps in the final. At this point, there was a growing sense that perhaps Wigan could do the unthinkable and beat Bath at union.

So when the game kicked off, the Bath forwards tore into Wigan, putting them on the back foot from the word go. To no-one's surprise, Wigan couldn't cope with scrummaging power and the first try of the match was a penalty try when Wigan repeatedly infringed at a scrum on their line. Jon Sleightholme then scored direct from a scrum when he burst through a weak Jason Robinson tackle. Bath scored two more tries and it was 25-0 at half-time.

But it was not the massacre that took place in the league match. Wigan were without their most important player, Shaun Edwards, and played the retired Lydon at fly-half with 42-year-old coach Graeme West in the second row. Three-quarter Inga Tuigamala spent the first half at open-side flanker.

When the second half kicked off Bath's forwards once again took control and two quick tries took them out of sight.

How Wigan v Bath Showed How Rugby Had Changed...

But Wigan then started to move the ball around and scored two tries in classic rugby league fashion. Bath stepped up the forward power and scored a pushover try before Wigan went the length of the field to make the final score 44-19 and draw the second half, beaten but not humiliated.

So league team wins league match and union team wins union match. Nothing much to see here. However, the whole affair was actually a fascinating insight into how the cultures of 19th century rugby remain very much alive.

For union, the fact that Wigan scored so many tries did not mean they were the better team: the key test was they coped with scrummaging and set-piece play. In this, you could hear the echo of Arthur Budd from 1888, who argued 'try-getters are plentiful' and valued goals far more than any touchdown.

In contrast, rugby league supporters were mystified by the emphasis of the union side on scrums. They believed, as Yorkshire's James Miller said in 1892 that 'the end of the "pushing age" had been reached and instead of admiring the physique and pushing power of those giants which took part in the game in the early stages... in the future they would be able to admire the skilful and scientific play of the game.'[1]

The cross-code matches also highlighted how rugby culture had inverted traditional class stereotypes.

Working-class people were usually portrayed as not being intellectual, preferring physical labour over mental tasks. In short, brawn over brain. Yet in union, the brawny, physical effort of scrummaging was superior to league's hand-eye co-ordination, combination play and quick-thinking tries.

Skills that would normally be seen as the epitome of grace and style if they came from a socially elite player were viewed as simple and unsophisticated when demonstrated by league players. In contrast, collective pushing and unseen violence (the so-called 'dark arts of the scrum'), which in any other walk of life would be seen as a symbols of working-class physicality, were treated as the sporting equivalent of theoretical physics. This too had a long history. In 1899, Frank Mitchell claimed NU players relied on 'stamina and physique' in contrast to the 'intelligent player' of rugby union.[2]

So in the run-up to Twickenham there was much talk that Wigan wouldn't be able to cope with the complexities and nuances of the scrum. Their victory in the Middlesex Sevens had been ascribed to their professional levels of fitness, rather than the intelligent way in which they adapted their skill set to the new game. And even in the union match, Wigan's comeback in the second half was put down to their higher level of physical fitness, not their rugby intelligence.

Indeed, it is often claimed the reason why Bath did not defeat Wigan by a huge score in the union match was because they 'went easy' in the scrums. But Bath won virtually every scrum and line-out, and used the scrum as a weapon right to the end, scoring a pushover try in the last ten minutes.

Other than deliberately injuring Wigan's front-row, it's difficult to know how they could have been more dominant in the set-piece. That Bath went easy on the Wigan pack has become the accepted story of the Twickenham game, even though it isn't an accurate description of the match.

What actually happened is that Bath did not play a tight game by kicking and setting up constant scrums to starve Wigan of the ball. An attritional approach would have ruined the match as a spectacle and demonstrated just how grim the game could be when one side chose to grind down the other. So Bath implicitly accepted that league-style rugby was the more attractive option.

One strange aspect of the legacy of the 1996 cross-code challenge is that the story about Bath going easy is accepted by many in rugby league. Speaking on the twenty-fifth

How Wigan v Bath Showed How Rugby Had Changed...

anniversary of the game, Terry O'Connor, who played in the Wigan pack in both matches, told Sky Sports rugby league podcast how thankful he was that Bath went easy in the scrums, but barely mentioned that Wigan went down to eleven players in the league match or the magnificence of Wigan's win at Maine Road.

To some extent, this acceptance of the union narrative by league people highlights the level of deference towards union that still exists in league. It took Will Greenwood, a guest on the same Sky podcast, to point out how superior Wigan were in skills common to both games. Yet it was Maurice Lindsay, then RFL chief executive, who used the Twickenham match to call for the unification of the two sports, which could only mean league joining union, instead of highlighting how the two matches demonstrated their differences. Most bizarrely, in both matches, commentator Mike Stephenson constantly referred to 'Baaath,' rather than his normal northern pronunciation of Bath ... it goes without saying that he would never have been forgiven if he talked about 'Caaastleford'.

Reflecting on the cross-code challenge in *The Times*, Simon Barnes concluded by saying that the history of the division in rugby 'does not matter any more, save to social historians.'

Well, for this social historian at least, the lesson of the Bath-Wigan encounters of 1996 was that the past matters a lot, on and off the field, to both codes of rugby and their followers.

Whether we like it or not, rugby's great split continues to shape the way the two codes play the game and how they watch it. Indeed, to quote William Faulkner, for rugby 'the past is never dead, it's not even past.'

---

[1] *Yorkshire Post*, 9 Oct 1892.
[2] Frank Mitchell, 'Forward Play' in Montague Shearman (ed.), *Football* (London: 1899) p. 276.

28.

1-2-3-4! The Rise And Fall (And Rise?) Of Drop-Goals

Rugby league has never been afraid to change the rules of rugby. But perhaps the most surprising recent example of this was the 2021 decision of Australia's National Rugby League (NRL) to increase the value of a drop-goal (or field-goal as it's known down under) from one to two points when it is is kicked from beyond the forty-metre line.

Coincidentally, and probably unknown to the NRL rule-makers, 2021 was also the fiftieth anniversary of Australian rugby league reducing the value of all drop-goals from two points to one.

The year 2021 also saw rugby union's premier southern hemisphere competition, Super Rugby, introduce a new goal-line drop-out rule, for when an attacker is held up or knocks on in-goal, or a defender grounds a kicked ball in their in-goal area, similar to the rugby league rule. The drop-goal and the drop-kick were suddenly back in vogue in both codes.

1-2-3-4! The Rise And Fall (And Rise?) Of Drop-Goals

The drop-kick is an unusual skill because it is only really possible with an oval ball. It dates back to the earliest origins of rugby. In 1866, Rugby School rules defined it as 'letting the ball drop from your hands on to the ground and kicking it the very instant it rises', and this definition has been accepted by all oval ball codes ever since.

In Australia, the founders of Australian Rules used the same definition, and today's NFL rulebook defines it as 'a kick by a player who drops the ball and kicks it as, or immediately after, it touches the ground.' Unlike the simpler punt or place-kick, the drop-kick is an elegant combination of placement, timing and force.

From rugby's earliest times, the drop-kick was one of the most prized skills in the game. In *Tom Brown's School Days* one of the first things to happen to Tom when he arrives at Rugby is an initiation into 'the mysteries of "off-side", "drop-kicks", "punts", "places" and the other intricacies of the great science of football.'[1] Later on in the book, the captain of Tom's team warns his team-mates that 'fuddling about in the public-house, and drinking bad spirits, and punch, and such rot-gut stuff … won't make good drop-kickers or chargers of you, take my word for it.'[2] The high status of the drop-kick in the public school game could also be seen in the fact that Marlborough College even awarded a special prize cap for drop-kicking every season from 1854.

During the first decades of rugby, drop-kicking was not only a way to score goals, but also the most important type of attacking kick in general play. Because rugby balls in the 19th century were larger and rounder, drop-kicking was more accurate and powerful than punting out of the hand.

However, by the 1880s the drop-kick in general play began to decline in importance. Defences had become quicker and there was less time to drop-kick deep into an opponent's half as players began to be given defensive assignments and acquired greater tactical sophistication. In 1896, rugby journalist and friend of Arthur Conan Doyle, Bertram Robinson, told his readers that punting 'is the only safe form of kick available for a back when he is penned by the advancing forwards of the other side.'

In contrast, while drop-kicking in general play was falling out of favour, it was an increasingly important method of scoring a goal. Until 1886, the only way to score in rugby was by doing just that. Matches were decided by the number of goals kicked by each team. Tries did not count as a scoring method but merely allowed a team to 'try' to kick a goal.

Goals could only be scored by a place-kick, a drop-kick or a field-goal, which was when a loose ball on the ground was kicked between the goal posts and over the bar (which is why it is technically incorrect to call a drop-goal a 'field-goal'). Field-goals were abolished in rugby union in 1905 but not until 1950 in rugby league – although the last field goal scored in a major rugby league match was in 1905 when Hull KR centre Billy Phipps kicked one in Rovers' 1905 Challenge Cup semi-final win over Broughton Rangers.

But in 1886, under pressure from the northern rugby clubs who favoured a more open game, the RFU introduced a points scoring system. Goals (including converted tries) were worth three points and an unconverted try was worth one point. Three years later, the RFU allowed goals to be kicked from penalties, and penalty goals were awarded two points. In 1891 the system was changed again, so unconverted tries were worth two points, penalty goals were three points, and drop-goals increased in value to four points. Drop-goals were now the single most valuable way of scoring.

The RFU leadership was not alone in believing that the drop-goal was the most valuable scoring method. In 1886,

1-2-3-4! The Rise And Fall (And Rise?) Of Drop-Goals

Canadian football, which was slowly evolving beyond rugby rules, introduced its first points system. A try was worth one point, a conversion two points and a dropped goal three.

So why had drop-goals become so important? As with so many other things in rugby, the answer can be found in the struggle in rugby between the predominantly working-class clubs in the north of England, and the clubs that controlled the RFU. In the north, where the game had become a mass spectator sport, the emphasis had shifted from a kicking-based game aimed at scoring goals to a handling game that put a premium on tries.

The northern rugby community believed a scoring system that valued goals above tries made the game unattractive for spectators to watch and for players to play. When the RFU increased the points awarded to penalties in 1888 the *Yorkshire Post* explained that:

> ...the acme of good play is when a skilful player finishes up a run in which passing plays a prominent part by dashing over the line and planting the ball between the posts ... dropping at goal is sadly overdone and for that reason we cannot but think the Union have placed too high a premium upon individual skill as against the combination of 15 men.[3]

In contrast, RFU president Arthur Budd spoke for many in the RFU leadership when he expressed the opposite view:

> The very fact that try-getters are plentiful while goal-droppers are scarce shows that the latter art is very much more difficult of acquirement ... why, I should like to ask, ought the more skilful piece of play to be depreciated, while a premium is placed on mere speed of foot?[4]

This was a widespread attitude in rugby union, and the drop-goal was worth four points until 1948, when it was reduced to its present three points.

In contrast, one of the major rule changes that the Northern Union made in 1897 was to reduce the value of the drop-goal and penalty-goal to just two points, while tries were kept at three points. For the first time in rugby history, tries were worth more than goals.

Rugby league's scoring system remained unchanged for seventy-six years, until the drop-goal was reduced to just one point in 1971. This reform was introduced because of the shift to four-tackle rugby in 1966. The limited number of tackles available to a team meant that it was now more difficult to get near an opponents' try line. So drop-kicking for goal from 30 or 40 metres out became a major tactic.

For example, when South Sydney beat Manly 23-12 in the 1970 New South Wales Grand Final – the match famous for Souths' John Sattler playing almost the entire game with a badly-broken jaw – Souths full-back Eric Simms kicked four drop-goals, while Manly's Bob Fulton kicked two. And in the 1971 Challenge Cup Final Alex Murphy's Leigh beat Leeds 24-7, not least thanks to four drop-goals.

But being able to win a match by scoring more goals than your opponent seemed to be against everything rugby league stood for, so the Australians halved the value of the drop-goal to one point in 1971. In Britain the rule was changed in 1974.

As a tactic to shift the score to more than a converted try by a team leading a match, the drop-goal became a vital if sparsely used skill. Introduction of 'Golden Point' sudden-death extra-time in the NRL and British Super League also increased the marginal importance of the one-pointer.

As a game strategy, 'drive and drop' never died out in rugby union, best remembered perhaps by Clive Woodward's World Cup-winning England team of 2003,

1-2-3-4! The Rise And Fall (And Rise?) Of Drop-Goals

although outside of South Africa it has faded over the last decade or so. Rugby union's 2019 World Cup saw just six drop-goals scored in the entire tournament, in contrast to the twenty-one kicked in 1999.

In the gridiron game, drop-kicks had long ago disappeared from the playing field, if not rulebook. The great quarterback Doug Flutie famously kicked a drop-goal for New England Patriots to score an extra point in his last ever NFL game in 2006, the first time that had been done since the 1941 Championship game. Nate Ebner, the ex-American Olympic rugby union sevens player, used a drop-kick to kick off for New England against Philadelphia in 2015, but effectively the drop-kick has gone the way of the dodo in the NFL. The same is true in the Canadian Football League.

The NRL decision to raise the value of the drop-goal kicked from outside the 40-metre line meant for the first time in 130 years, one of the rugby codes has raised its value. Can the drop-goal make a comeback in the sport that originally rejected its importance? It seems unlikely, but if it becomes anything more than a novelty scoring method, the weight of generations of rugby league tradition will soon start to bear down on the NRL's leaders and change will be in the air.

Even when it comes to drop-goals, no sport, not even the NRL, can escape from its own history.

---

[1] *Tom Brown's School Days*, p. 99.
[2] *Tom Brown's School Days*, p.123.
[3] *Yorkshire Post*, 7 Jan 1888.
[4] Arthur Budd, 'The Northern Union' in *Football* (London: 1897) p. 34.

29.

Imitation Is Not Just A Form Of Flattery: Why Union Borrows From League

In 2021, rugby union's international governing body, World Rugby, introduced the 50-22. The new rule meant that if a player kicked the ball from their own half and it bounced into touch within the opposition's 22, the kicking team received a line-out.

As everyone in both codes pointed out, the rule was based on rugby league's 40-20, whereby the side that kicks a ball from behind their 40 metre line and which bounces into touch behind their opponents' 20-metre line, retains possession.

League fans claimed it was one more example of union stealing from league and rugby union critics denounced it too, for bringing their game closer to the thirteen-a-side version. An article by Stuart Barnes in *The Times* was headlined 'League Gimmick Is Just Dumbing Down', which demonstrated that some people still like to party like it's 1899.

In reality, the 50-22 is one more example of how rugby's

Imitation Is Not Just A Form Of Flattery

evolution inevitably means rugby union has borrowed, and will continue to borrow from rugby league.

This goes back to the Northern Union. In 1897, two years after rugby's great split, the NU, as we have seen, changed the scoring system to make tries more valuable than goals. In rugby union at that time, tries were worth three points, the same as penalty goals but less than drop-goals, which until 1948 were worth four points. The Northern Union reduced all goals to two points to put a premium on try-scoring, which it saw as rugby's most attractive feature.

For a long time, many in union still believed goal-kicking was the heart of the game. It wasn't until 1971, the centenary year of the Rugby Football Union, that the rule was changed to make tries worth four points, a point more than a penalty or drop-goal. However, even that reform did not do enough to encourage try-scoring and so, in 1992, the value of a try was raised to five points.

Other rugby union rule changes often followed in league's wake. In the 1950s and 1960s, union became dominated by direct kicking into touch. The game became more competitive and teams found the most efficient way to win was to play ten-man rugby, and advance down the pitch by kicking to touch, winning the line-out, kicking to touch, winning the line-out, ad infinitum. When, in 1963, Wales beat Scotland at Murrayfield, this style of play resulted in 111 line-outs in the 80 minutes of the match.

In 1970, to bring an end to such brain-numbing tactics, the International Rugby Board outlawed direct kicking into touch from outside the 25 yard line (today's 22 metre line). This did open up the game, which became increasingly important as international rugby union became a staple of TV networks.

Once again, though, rugby league had long since penalised direct kicking into touch; in 1902 to be precise.

By this time league had also abolished the line-out, largely on the grounds that, as Oliver Cromwell said about the House of Lords, it was useless and dangerous. Abolition of the line-out had also been discussed in union, because while it is now a treasured part of the game, it was not always so. In 1972, the RFU's laws committee even discussed abolishing it. The 1999 legalisation of lifting in the line-out, previously seen as a heinous form of cheating, has changed completely the nature of the set-piece, with the ball being retained by the throwing side approximately 90 per cent of the time.

Even today's rugby union rules, which allow the tackled player to release the ball backwards, have taken union significantly down the road of league's play-the-ball, allowing the attacking side to retain possession over 90 per cent of the time, according to World Rugby's analysis of the 2021 Six Nations. The 'struggle for possession' in rugby union, is slowly disappearing, just as it has in league.

Off the pitch, rugby union has also followed league. The Northern Union introduced shirt numbering in 1911, and the International Rugby Board (forerunner of World Rugby), in 1960 eventually did the same, although it decided to reverse the numbering of players. League introduced substitutes in 1964, while union followed with 'replacements' in 1970. League borrowed the sin-bin from ice hockey in 1983, which union borrowed from league in 2000. Super League brought the video ref to rugby in 1996, which union followed in 2001. English rugby union didn't have a national knock-out cup until 1971, nor a league system until 1987, both of which had been a staple of league since its earliest days.

The most significant rule changes in rugby league came in two waves. The first was the series of reforms in the decade following the split with rugby union, which gave the Northern Union's evolutionary impulses the freedom to develop the game as a spectacle, led to the changes to scoring to emphasise tries and open, running rugby.

The second wave of change came at the start of the sports' television age in the 1960s, when limited-tackle rugby was introduced and the ambiguity of the rules around the scrum and play-the-ball was removed, the contest for possession being gradually replaced by a struggle for territory.

Each of these rule changes were responses to specific problems. The first wave of changes sought to promote the scoring of tries and reduce the traditional importance of scrums and goal-kicking. Thirteen-a-side meant there was more room on the pitch for running rugby, and the play-the-ball speeded up games.

The second wave was also a response to how coaches and players had found ways of slowing the game down. So in 1966 the four-tackle rule was introduced to stop one side having endless play-the-balls, known as the 'creeping barrage', and killing off a match they led. In 1972 this became six tackles to allow for more creative play.

In union, there has essentially been one big evolutionary spurt since the late 1980s when it was realised professionalism was coming and union needed to become a product for TV. There has been an almost continuous push to improve the game's entertainment value, from the legalisation of lifting in the line-out to reforming the ruck and the maul to ensure more open play. In 1995, there were even experimental games of thirteen-a-side played in Scotland.

Professionalism also increased the speed of union. Scrums and line-outs have been drastically reduced, but the number of tackles, and thus mauls and rucks, has risen. The number of passes has risen too, while kicking has fallen. Penalty goals have decreased, but try-scoring has increased, all at a rate of change since 1995 greater than for an entire previous century.

But rugby union has not finished its transformation. Like league in the 1960s, it too suffers from endless 'phases' of tackling and recycling the ball. Indeed, for those old enough to remember, modern union is not unlike league as played in the 1950s and 1960s. It will not be too long before we hear calls to restrict the number of phases a team can have.

The scrum will continue to wither in importance, not least because of the time it takes. World Rugby's own statistics show that at the knockout stages of its 2019 World Cup, scrums took up an average of 18 per cent of ball-in-play time, almost a fifth of the match. And there will eventually be a debate on the number of players in a team – using defensive systems adapted from a game for 13 players will eventually suffocate a game with 15 players on the field.

Is union going down this path simply because it wants to steal rugby league's ideas? It's not that simple.

For a start, as the 50-22 controversy demonstrated yet again, some in union still think league is a dirty word.

But, ultimately, union will have no choice but to follow a similar path to league. It is currently trying to solve the same problems that rugby league has been trying to do for the last 125 years. And in reality there are only a limited set of solutions if you want retain the fundamentals of rugby.

Aussie Rules began as rugby, but quickly abandoned off-side and rule changes cascaded from there. American football still saw itself as part of the rugby family until it too amended the off-side rule in 1906 to legalise the forward pass. Unless rugby union ditches one or more of the basic principles of rugby, such as off-side or the scrum, it has no other course but to follow rugby league.

This also explains why league has borrowed almost nothing from union. League has long since moved along the evolutionary path from the position where union is today.

Imitation Is Not Just A Form Of Flattery

Indeed, it looks to other sports, with the idea of limited tackle rugby coming directly from American football's 'four downs' system.

There is, however, one emerging factor that will force both codes to come up with new solutions. That is the concussion crisis, the discovery of the terrible and terrifying effects of head injuries on players.

Although rugby union is going down the same road rugby league has already taken, this does not mean they will merge, because the two sports travel it in very different vehicles. Tradition weighs heavily on both, in the ways they play rugby and in how they see the game. Rugby's great split of 1895 created two separate and distinct sports on and off the pitch, and culturally they could not be further apart.

These two cultures have remained constant ever since they appeared at the end of the 19th century. Each code of rugby brings not just recreation, but also meaning and identity to the lives of hundreds of thousands of people and the communities to which they belong.

After all, sport is about much more than just sport itself – and the evolution of rugby is also about much more than what is written in a rulebook.

30.

The Game That Won't Die: Why Reports Of Rugby League's Death Have Been Greatly Exaggerated

Does rugby league have a future? Crowds are declining, playing standards are sinking and the administration of the game is in crisis. The Test match between Great Britain and Australia played at Wembley Stadium attracted just 9,874 people, a humiliating crowd for a match broadcast live on national television. There is no wonder that Hull KR official Ron Chester said: 'Rugby league isn't dying, it's dead.'

But of course, this isn't the state of rugby league today. It's actually a snapshot of the British game in the early 1970s, when many people inside and outside of the sport were predicting it would only be a matter of time before the last rites were read.

Things were almost as bad as they sounded. As a ten-year old in 1971, I watched New Zealand win the series against Great Britain in front of just 4,108 people at Castleford. But, over fifty years later, the game hasn't died and is far healthier

The Game That Won't Die

than it was when I was in short trousers. In fact, the claim that rugby league is dying has been around since the sport was born.

Just five weeks after the founding meeting at the George Hotel in 1895, the London newspaper *Pall Mall Gazette* confidently predicted that 'in a year or two, the Northern Union will almost be forgotten.' The game's survival back then made little difference to the doom-mongers. In January 1907, the *Halifax Courier* reported that a rival newspaper had proclaimed 'Northern Union dying' on one of its advertising posters.

Nor was the sport given much hope in Australia.

In August 1907, Sydney sports paper *The Arrow* predicted that rugby league in Sydney would be 'nothing more but a nine day wonder', and that anyone who played the game would 'commit football suicide.'

The belief that rugby league was only a short step away from death has become what sociologists call a meme: an idea that grows by constant repetition and takes on a life of its own, regardless of whether it is true or false. The fact that the evidence doesn't support the meme is irrelevant.

After all, the Northern Union, albeit under a different name since 1922, has far out-lived both the *Pall Mall Gazette* and *The Arrow*. And just two months after the *Halifax Courier* article, the sport made its biggest breakthrough when Albert Baskerville wrote to the Northern Union to tell them he was establishing the game in New Zealand.

But the idea that rugby league was at death's door was not extinguished by reference to reality. In 1934, Sydney's *Daily Telegraph* asked: 'Is rugby league doomed?' And not to be outdone, London's *Daily Telegraph* in its report on the 1954 World Cup final said that 'rugby league is still dying.'

The repeated failure of league to expire did nothing to stop the spread of the meme. In his 1973 autobiography, former All Black captain and New Zealand politician Chris Laidlaw told his readers that rugby league, except in Australia, was dying. There was little hope for it there either, Laidlaw argued, because it was being overtaken by soccer.

In 1979, rugby union journalist John Reason gazed into his crystal ball and declared that 'the game of rugby league will itself die, it has become quite pathetic.' In the early 1990s, as rugby union lurched towards professionalism, *Sunday Times* reporter Stephen Jones made his own bid to become the Nostradamus of the oval ball: 'I predict the death of Rugby League,' he informed his readers.

The legalisation of open professionalism in rugby union in 1995 led many journalists to claim that league had no future. Most notoriously, in 2001, Frank Keating of *The Guardian* prematurely wrote its epitaph, which began: 'Great game rugby league. Such a shame it has to die.' The success of the 2003 Rugby World Cup in Australia also led to a hailstorm of articles predicting the demise of rugby league in Australia.

It's worth noting that academic sports sociologists were at the forefront of such predictions. Professor David Rowe confidently told his Tom Brock lecture audience in 2006 that 'rugby league is the most vulnerable of the football codes in Australia' and that it would soon fall behind soccer and rugby union because 'it was the code with the slightest prospects for future prosperity.' And one very well known Australian sports studies professor confidently told me in 2000 that 'rugby league is gone, mate.' Quite.

It's not too difficult to see why the 'rugby league is dying' meme survived. Partly it was due to the wishful thinking of some people in rugby union, who mistook their desires for reality. They believed that rugby league had no right to exist, and therefore assumed it would inevitably die.

The Game That Won't Die

For the less cynical, there was also an ignorance about league, with many in union simply assuming that it was little more than a professional version of their own game. So they believed professionalism in union would inevitably lead to the end of league. Those who held this view knew little about rugby league and had no understanding of the deep roots and cultural significance it has for its communities.

There was also a degree of social snobbery in this attitude. After all, once both games became professional, wouldn't rugby league people defer to the socially superior code and accept its leadership? This was a long-standing aspect of union's attitude to league. The mere existence of the 13-a-side code was an affront to the hierarchical worldview of union's leaders, and league's disappearance would confirm the correctness of their views. But the plebeian leaguies were not inclined to accept this inevitability.

It was not just league's opponents who predicted its death, however. The meme has also been accepted by some league supporters and officials. The defection of Manningham and Bradford from league to soccer in the 1900s was motivated in part by their officials' belief that the Northern Union was on its last legs. In the 1960s, as crowds started to decline and finances plummeted, rugby league's navel-gazing turned to its own mortality. This led to Ron Chester's infamous 1971 statement that rugby league had in fact already snuffed it.

Despite the obvious fact that the game did not die, the meme continued to reappear whenever the sport was felt to be in crisis. Problems with the game's leadership, declining crowd numbers and international issues always seem to be terminal. The fact that the same set of questions constantly reappear illustrates not the end of rugby league, but its deep-seated structural problems and failure to find long-term solutions.

Of course, the game has also struggled for decades to find leaders with the breadth of experience and strategic vision to take it forward. But so too have other major sports. It is also worth remembering that in the 1950s and 1960s, the RFL was run by Bill Fallowfield, a man who spent considerable time trying to re-introduce rugby union rules to the game.

So while rugby league crowds have declined since the late 2000s, they are still historically higher than at any time since the mid-1960s And although international rugby league is in dire need of strong direction, the sport has never been played by more nations, nor had as many participants around the world. Without comparing the present with previous eras or other sports, any difficulties are easily interpreted as terminal. And of course, the media thrives on simplistic stories, sensational headlines and clickbait.

Could rugby league die? Of course, it's not impossible, but none of the major sports established in the great sporting boom of the late 19th century have disappeared. League's deep social and cultural roots, combined with the passion for the game of hundreds of thousands of people, will keep it alive, as they have other football codes.

But rugby league could be increasingly marginalised. One of the ways that might happen is if it loses its self-confidence and sense of purpose, and becomes perceived as a sport constantly in conflict with itself, and unsure of its place in the world. Such an image will not inspire loyalty, nor offer an attractive image in the 21st century world of Instagram, TikTok and social media.

Positive change in any sport must be based on a sense of pride and self confidence in its heritage and history. In fact, far from being on the verge of death, the real story is of rugby league surviving against the odds, despite more than a century of institutional discrimination.

The Game That Won't Die

Rugby union, for all its best efforts, wasn't able to kill off league; and indeed it has itself survived by adopting many of rugby league's rules.

Nor did the fratricidal Super League war of the 1990s inflict a mortal wound.

And of course, not even the combined forces of French rugby union and the fascistic Vichy government of war time France, could ultimately kill the game there. So the meme that rugby league is dying is simply plain wrong.

In fact, one of league's most outstanding features is not that it is always on the verge of extinction, but on the contrary that, often under extraordinarily difficult circumstances and tremendous pressures, the code has survived – and often thrived – for over 125 years and counting.

Long may it continue!

Index

Abertillery: 43
Alcock, Charles: 29, 32
Alexandra Athletic Club: 140
Amateur Athletic Association: 28, 128
Amateurism: 7, 19, 20, 27-33, 35-38, 46, 47, 56-58, 60, 61, 63, 68, 80-85, 96, 98, 99, 113, 118, 128-130, 134, 139, 145, 148, 150
American Football: 11, 74, 75, 78, 109, 134, 135, 136, 157, 161, 166, 167
Amos & Smith (Hull): 119
Anderson, Lindsay: 121, 126
Andrews, Sybil: 104
Ardwick FC: 64, 66, 69
Arnold, Thomas: 72, 74
Ashbourne: 91
Athletics: 28, 119, 139, 140
Auckland (New Zealand): 44, 53, 61
Australia: 1, 3, 7, 9, 43-44, 53, 54-58, 59-63, 73, 130, 132, 156, 157, 169, 170
Australian rugby union: 53, 54-58, 59, 60, 62, 78, 170
Australian rugby league: 53, 54-58, 130, 156, 160, 169, 170
National Rugby League (NRL): 132, 156, 160, 161
Australia rugby league men's national team: 57, 130, 168
Australian Rules football: 9, 11, 55, 57, 61-62, 75, 76, 109, 138, 157, 166
Aviron Bayonnaise: 107

Badel, Alan: 125
Banks, Lucius: 133-137
Barbarians RFC: 83
Barnes, Stuart: 162
Barraclough, Alf: 87
Barrow-in-Furness: 42
Barrow RLFC: 135, 141
Barry Island: 43
Baskerville, Albert: 130, 169
Bath RFC: 150-155
Batley: 34, 141
Batley RLFC: 35, 40, 140, 141
Batten, Billy: 135, 136
Batty, Grant: 78
Baumeister, Willi: 104
Baxter, James: 94, 95
BBC: 34, 70, 95
Bedell-Sivright, David: 50

Bevan, Brian: 130
Birkinshaw: Sam: 130
Birmingham: 82
Blaby (Leicestershire): 80
Black players in rugby league: 127, 133-137
Blackburn Olympic: 19, 31, 65
Blackburn Rovers: 31, 65
Blackheath FC: 21, 61, 83
Blaina (Wales): 34
Bloxam, Matthew: 6
Boardman, Isabella: 40
Boccioni, Umberto: 104
Bolton: 65, 66
Boot money: 38
Boston, Billy: 130
Bowen, Harry: 35
Boxing: 52, 127, 128, 132
Bradford: 82, 89, 151
Odsal: 151
Park Avenue: 89, 90
Bradford FC: 26, 87, 136, 140, 171
Bramley FC: 77, 98, 132, 140
Brisbane: 55, 57, 62
Bristol RFC: 135, 147
British & Irish Rugby Union Lions: 59, 63
British Football Association: 30, 31
British Ladies FC: 41
Broadbent, George: 98
Brock, Tom: 170
Brodetsky, Selig: 131
Broken time: 8, 29, 30, 32, 118
Broughton Rangers: 36, 40, 67-69, 128-130, 158
'Mrs Boardman's Boys': 40
Brown, Tony: 76
Budd, Arthur: 31, 93, 153, 159
Burnley AFC: 19, 65
Burton RFC: 82
Bury: 66
Bush, Percy: 106, 107
Byrne, James: 84

Cail, William: 82
Calcutta Cup: 18, 20
Callard, Jon: 152
Cambridge University: 12, 46, 47, 60, 61
Camp, Walter: 74
Canada: 7, 73
Canadian Rules Football: 11, 75, 109, 159, 161
Caracostea, Gregore: 145

Cardiff: 35, 36, 43, 106
Cardiff Arms Park: 43
Cardiff RFC: 2, 23, 36, 51, 103-108, 147
Cardiff women's rugby union: 43
Carlton FC (Melbourne): 61
Castleford: 124, 132, 141, 168
Catt, Mike: 152
C.D. Holmes (Hull): 118
Charnley, Tom: 65
Cheltenham College: 115
Chester, Ron: 168, 171
Chorley FC: 65, 66
Christchurch (New Zealand): 44
Cleckheaton FC: 140
Clowes, Jack: 60-62
Coen, Darren: 132
Concussion: 167
Cooper, Fred: 87, 89
Corinthians FC: 9, 30
Cornwall: 51, 129
Coubertin, Pierre de: 74
Coventry RFC: 81, 82, 84, 85
Coventry City: 81
Crane, Arnold: 84
Cricket: 8, 16, 29, 60, 61, 71, 77, 98, 101, 111, 117, 119, 138, 140
Crockwell, James: 106
Crowds/spectators: 7, 16, 20, 23, 24, 30, 35, 40, 41, 43, 44, 48, 58, 62, 66-68, 77, 81, 86, 87, 90, 92, 100, 104-106, 108, 113, 116, 118-120, 121, 141, 142, 159, 168, 171, 172
Crumbie, Tom: 83-85
Curran, George: 137
Cwmbran (Wales): 43
Czechoslovakia: 145

Dalgleish, Adam: 139
Darwen FC: 17, 18, 28
Dawkins, Pete: 78
Dawson, Victoria Samantha: 42
Deans, Bob: 52
Dearham Amazons (Cumbria): 44
Delaney, Shelagh: 123
Delaunay, Robert, 103-108
Derby: 80
Devon: 50
Dewsbury: 140-142
Dewsbury FC: 35, 36, 140

175

Index

Dick, Kerr Ladies FC: 39
Dixon, Colin: 34
Dobson, Tommy: 87
Doubleday, Abner: 9
Douglas (Isle Of Man): 60
Doyle, Arthur Conan: 2, 45-48, 87, 158
Dublin: 46
Durham: 51, 89

Earle's Engineers (Hull): 116
Eastern Suburbs (Sydney): 55, 130
Ebner, Nate: 161
Edinburgh: 60, 104, 139
 Murrayfield: 163
Edwards, Shaun: 152
Eley, Maria: 43
Ellis, William Webb: 1, 5-10, 41
Enderby (Leicestershire): 80
Eton College: 12, 14, 71, 91
Everton FC: 90

FA Cup: 7, 15, 16-21, 29-31, 65, 67, 82, 89, 99
Fallowfield, Bill: 148, 172
Featherstone: 42
Fédération Internationale de Rugby Amateur: 145
Fihelly, Jack: 57
Five (later Six) Nations Championship: 34, 79, 95, 96, 106, 113, 145, 149, 164
Fletcher, Raymond: 123
Flutie, Doug: 161
Follis, Charles: 135
Football (folk): 7, 75, 80, 91
Football Association: 6, 7, 12, 15, 17-20, 28-32, 67, 70, 74, 75-77
Football League: 19, 20, 56, 65, 67, 99, 101, 131
France: 74, 95, 103-108, 136, 144, 145, 149, 173
France rugby union: 74, 95, 107, 109, 145, 149, 173
Fulton, Bob: 160
Fursac, Joseph Rogues de: 106

Gaelic Football: 11, 75
Galashiels: 139
Gallaher, Dave: 52
Garnett, Harry: 8
George Hotel (Huddersfield): 24-25, 169
Germany: 54, 145
Gilbert, William: 13, 14

Glasgow: 41
Glasgow Rangers FC: 140
Glaskie, Reuben: 129
Glebe-Balmain RUFC: 56
Gleizes, Albert: 104, 105
Gloucester RFC: 147
Godsell, Vanda: 125
Gold, Max: 130
Goldthorpe, Albert: 136
Goole: 117
Gould, Arthur: 37
Great Britain Rugby League Lions: 60, 63, 122, 130, 168
Greenberg, Todd: 132
Greenwood, Will: 155
Guillemard, Arthur: 23, 92, 111
Gurdon, Charles: 92
Gwyn, Dai: 36

Haig, Ned: 140
Halifax: 25, 61, 94, 121
Hallaton Bottle-Kicking Game: 11, 80
Harding, Rowe, 146-148
Harlequins RFC: 147, 149
Harris, Louis: 130
Harris, Richard: 121-124
Harrison, Gilbert: 115
Harrow School: 12, 71
Hawick: 60, 139
Haxey Hood: 12
Heckmondwike: 88, 116, 141
Heisman Trophy: 78
Henry, Joe: 98, 99, 102
Hickie, Tom: 58
Hill, Rowland: 18, 37, 60, 85, 86, 87, 112
Holbeck FC: 97-102, 129
Holmfirth: 81
Horbury FC: 40
Hornby (New Zealand): 44
Huddersfield: 8, 24, 42, 81, 87, 97, 100, 130, 140. 141
Hughes, Thomas: 45, 70-74
 Tom Brown's School Days: 2, 45, 70-74, 157
Hull: 83, 115-120, 128, 131
 Boothferry Park: 119
 Boulevard/Hull Athletic Ground: 119
 Craven Street ground: 119
 Craven Park: 130
 Hull & District Rugby Union: 120
 Hull City AFC: 119
 Hull FC: 26, 35, 115-120, 132
 Hull Kingston Rovers: 115-120, 123, 130, 158, 168
Hunslet: 99, 100, 101, 129, 135, 137
Hunslet RLFC: 94, 98, 129, 133-136
Hunter, Jimmy: 50
Hutchinson, William H.H.: 115-116

Injuries: 160, 167
International Rugby Football Board (later World Rugby): 5, 37, 59, 79, 95, 96, 113, 148, 150, 162-164, 166
Ireland: 7, 41, 51, 57, 58, 83
Isle of Man: 60
Italy: 104, 113, 145

Jackson, F.S.: 84
Jackson, N.L.: 29, 32
Jacobson, Eli: 129
James, Carwyn: 146
James, David: 36, 129
James, Evan: 36, 129
Jewish community: 127-132
 Anti-Semitism: 128, 131
 Ashkenazi Jews: 132
 Hull Judeans RLFC: 131
 Judean Social Sports Club (Sydney): 131
 Leeds Judeans RL: 131
 Maccabean Sport & Athletic Club (Sydney): 131
 Maccabi Institute (Sydney): 131
 Sabbath: 129, 130, 131
 Young Persons Hebrew Association (Sydney): 131
 Zionism: 131
Johnson, Simon: 132
Jones, Stephen: 170

Keating, Frank: 170
Keighley RLFC: 100
Kelso RFC: 139
Keneally, Thomas: 3

Laidlaw, Chris: 170
Lalanne, Denis: 95
Lambert, Charles Beevor: 115
Lancashire (county): 17, 19, 29, 30, 35, 36, 46, 64-69, 77, 141
Lancashire FA Cup: 65
Lancashire Rugby Union: 19, 65, 67, 142
Lancashire Cup (rugby union): 66

176

Index

Lancashire county rugby union team: 40, 47, 86, 88, 89
Larkin, Ted: 57
Leeds: 16, 83, 97-102, 121, 128, 129, 131, 136, 141
  Cardigan Arms: 16
  Elland Road Stadium/Holbeck Recreation Ground: 98, 99, 101, 102
  Headingley: 16, 131, 151
  Peacock Inn: 99
Leeds City AFC: 100-102
Leeds FC: 71
Leeds Parish Church FC: 128, 129, 140
Leeds St John's (Leeds Rhinos): 25, 65, 98, 122, 129, 131, 132, 140, 141, 160
Leeds United: 2, 97-102, 129
Lees, Sam: 87
Lieberman Cup (Sydney): 131
Leicester: 80-85
Leicester City AFC: 81
Leicestershire: 11, 80, 81
Leicester Tigers: 80-85, 147, 151
Leigh: 26, 42, 160
Levy, Edward: 128
Lhote, André: 105
Lincolnshire: 12
Lindsay, Maurice: 155
Lindon, Rebecca: 14
Lindon, Richard: 14, 15
Liverpool: 16, 19
Liverpool FC: 65, 68
Lockwood, Dicky: 88, 89
London: 7, 8, 13, 29, 64, 73, 83, 84, 98, 122, 127, 169,
Lowe, Arthur: 125
Luric, Stanislav: 147
Lydon, Joe: 152

MacGregor, Duncan: 50, 51
Manchester (city of): 2, 16, 19, 30, 36, 64-69, 89, 128, 130, 131, 151
  Fallowfield: 67, 89, 90
  Maine Road: 151, 155
  The Cliff: 69
  Whalley Range: 65
Manchester City AFC: 64
Manchester FA: 67
Manchester FC: 64, 65, 68
Manchester United AFC: 64, 69
Mănescu, Manea: 145

Manly RLFC: 160
Manly RUFC: 55
Manningham FC: 82, 87, 171
Manson, Barney: 130
Marshall, Reverend Frank: 9, 40, 46, 59
Marsh Blondes (Workington): 44
Mawson, Swan & Morgan: 88, 90
McCutcheon, Bill: 35, 36, 87
McKenna, John: 65
Melrose: 138-143
Metropolitan Blues RLFC (women): 43
Metropolitan Cup (Sydney): 56
Metzinger, Jean: 104
Middlesex Sevens: 142, 152, 154
Midland Counties RFU: 82, 83
Miller, James: 24, 86, 93, 153
Mitchell, Frank: 8, 77, 154
Moloney, Maggie: 43
Morgan, Teddy: 52, 107
Morgan, Thomas: 88
Morgan, William (Billy Bordeaux): 107
Moseley FC: 82, 84
Mosman RUFC: 55
Murphy, Alex: 160

Native New Zealand Team (1888-1889): 49
Neath: 35
Nevinson, Christopher: 104
Newcastle (Australia): 55
Newcastle (UK): 16, 88, 90
Newport: 35, 37, 43, 51, 52
Newsome, Mark: 36
New South Wales: 55-58, 62, 160
Newton Abbot: 50
Newton Heath AFC: 64, 66, 69
New Zealand: 44, 49-53, 59-63, 73, 78, 94, 131, 169, 170
New Zealand All Blacks: 49-53, 78, 93-95, 106, 107, 109, 170
New Zealand rugby league touring teams: 52, 53, 77, 168
Nicholl, Joe: 25
Northampton FC: 81, 84, 85
Northampton Town: 81
Northern Rugby Football Union: 8, 15, 20, 22, 24-26, 37, 38, 42, 43, 47, 48, 51, 60,

68, 77, 84, 85, 87, 88, 90, 93, 94, 98-100, 120, 154, 160, 163, 164, 169, 171
North Sydney RUFC: 55
Nottinghamshire: 60
Nuneaton RFC: 81
Nuneaton Town: 81

O'Connor, Terry: 155
Offiah, Martin: 151
Old Etonians FC: 7, 17, 28, 31
Oldham: 35, 36, 66-68, 87
Old Rugbeian Society: 6, 7
Olympic Games: 74, 138, 145, 147, 161
Otley RUFC: 90
Oxford University: 7, 46, 47, 78

Paris: 103, 107, 144, 145
Parr, Lily: 39, 40, 41, 44
Pendlebury RLFC: 134
Peters, Jimmy: 135
Phillips, Malcolm: 78
Phillips, R.J.: 113
Phipps, Billy: 158
Picasso, Pablo: 104, 107
Plymouth: 50, 135
Porter, Cliff: 94
Preoteasa, Grigore: 145, 147
Prescott, Alan: 63
Preston: 65, 66
Preston North End: 19, 29, 30, 65
Priest, William: 106, 107
Pritchard, Cliff: 52
Professionalism: 7, 8, 19, 20, 25, 27-33, 35-38, 47, 48, 49, 51, 53, 57, 59-63, 65, 67, 68, 77, 79, 84, 95, 96, 98, 100, 101, 112, 113, 118, 122, 124, 132, 133-137, 142, 147, 148, 150, 151, 154, 165, 170, 171
Pullin, A.W. (Old Ebor): 101

Quay Brunettes (Workington): 44
Queensland: 55, 56, 62
Queen's Park FC: 31

Racing Club de France: 145
Randwick RUFC: 55
Reason, John: 170
Reckitt & Sons: 118
Redman, Edward: 82
Revie, Don: 97
Richmond FC: 21, 83
Ritson, T.Y.: 65

177

Index

Rivière, Jacques: 105
Roberts, Glyn: 20
Roberts, Rachel: 121
Robinson, Bertram Fletcher: 20, 47, 48, 158
Robinson, Jason: 152
Rochdale: 67, 68
Rochdale Hornets: 130
Roe, Harry Owen: 107
Romania: 144-149
Roosevelt, Theodore: 74
Rosenberg, Wilf: 132
Rosenfeld, Albert: 129, 130
Rosten, Leo: 132
Rousseau, Henri: 104
Royal Engineers FC: 31
Rubin, Ian: 132
Rugby (Warwickshire): 5, 13
Rugby Football League (RFL): 132, 148, 155, 172
Rugby Football Union (RFU): 7, 8, 15, 17-21, 22, 23, 24-26, 28, 29, 31, 35-38, 47-49, 55, 56, 59-63, 67, 68, 76, 77, 82-85, 86, 92-95, 98, 110-113, 116, 118, 120, 141, 142, 147-149, 151, 158, 159, 163, 164
Rugby League Challenge Cup: 69, 90, 122, 128, 151, 158, 160
Rugby League World Cup: 169
Rugby School: 5-10, 12-14, 46, 70-74, 92, 109, 111, 115, 157
Rugby (Union) World Cup: 5, 109, 110, 113, 160, 161, 166, 170
Russell-Cargill, Dr J.A.: 142

Salford: 6, 8, 63
Salford RLFC: 41, 66-69, 131
Samuels, Lester: 130
Sattler, John: 160
Scotch Professors: 30
Scotland: 29, 30, 41, 60, 104, 107, 113, 138-143, 165
Scottish Rugby Union: 18, 51, 139, 163, 165
Section Paloise (France): 106
Seddon, Bob: 60-63
Selby: 116, 117
Sewell, Harry: 25
Shaw and Shrewsbury's Australian Team (1888): 59-62
Shaw, C.F.: 141
Shearman, Montague: 128
Sheffield: 42, 81

Sheffield Football Association: 75, 76
Sheffield FC: 75, 77
Shrewsbury School: 12
Shrove Tuesday: 6, 80, 91
Sillitoe, Alan: 123
Simms, Eric: 160
Simpson, Charles: 26
Sleightholme, Jon: 152
Smith, F.E. (Lord Birkenhead): 37
South Africa: 73, 78, 87, 149, 161
Springboks: 94, 95, 132
Southport: 66
South Shields RFC: 83
South Sydney RLFC: 132, 160
South Sydney RUFC: 55
Speedway: 131
Stadden, William (Buller): 36
Stade Bordelais: 106, 107
Stade Français: 107, 144
Stephenson, Mike: 155
St Helens: 39, 40, 42, 44
Knowsley Road: 39
St Helens Ladies FC: 39
St Helens RLFC: 26, 66, 97, 98, 101, 131
St Peter's School, York: 115
Stoddart, Andrew: 60-62
Stoker, Bram: 46
Stoneyhurst College: 46
Storey, David: 2, 121-126
Stuart, Angus: 36
Sudell, William: 29, 65
Sullivan, Clive: 34
Sullivan, Jim: 63
Sutcliffe, Charles: 65
Sutherland, A.A.: 8, 66
Swan, Joseph: 88
Swansea RFC: 35, 36, 51, 129, 146-148
Swinton RLFC: 40, 60, 64, 67, 68, 69, 84, 130
Sydney, Australia: 43, 55, 56, 58, 61, 62, 73, 129, 131, 132, 169
Sydney Reds RLFC (women): 43
Sydney University FC: 55

Tattersall, Sam: 84
Television: 79, 155, 163, 165, 168
Thomas, Clem: 146
Thomas, W.H.: 61
Thornes FC: 24, 93, 142
Toothill, Jack: 87

Toulouse: 107
Trail, Ken: 122, 124
Trinity College, Dublin: 46
Tuigamala, Inga: 152
Twickenham: 83, 121, 149, 152, 154, 155

Upton Park AFC: 29
USA: 7, 9, 73, 106, 124, 132, 133-137, 144, 145, 161
USSR: 87, 128, 145-148

Valentine, Emily: 41
Van Praag, Lionel: 131
Vichy: 173
Victoria (Australia): 55, 57, 58, 61, 62, 73

Wagstaff, Harold: 63, 130
Wakefield: 24, 116, 121, 122, 142
Wakefield Trinity: 21, 35, 65, 121-123, 140
Wakefield, William Wavell: 95, 110, 147, 148
Wales: 1, 23, 24, 34-38, 43, 51, 85, 103-108, 139, 146
Wales rugby union national men's team: 35-38, 52, 61, 83, 106, 107, 129, 139, 146, 149, 163
Warrington RLFC: 26, 66, 67
Wasps RFC: 152
Watkins, David: 34
Wellington (New Zealand): 50, 61
Welsh Rugby Union: 35-38
Wembley Stadium: 168
Werneth FC: 66
West, Graeme: 152
Whitehaven: 42
Whitehaven Recreation RLFC: 26
Widnes RLFC: 66
Wigan: 42, 43, 66, 68, 83
Wigan RLFC: 21, 66, 67, 122, 150-155
Williams, Tennessee: 124
Winchester School: 91
Winfield, Bert: 52
Wollen, William: 86-90, 103
Wolverhampton Wanderers: 89
Woodward, Clive: 160
Women: 39-44, 40, 41, 91, 137
Workington: 44
World War One: 41, 43, 54-58, 69, 87, 103-106, 136, 145

178

Index

World War Two: 56, 129, 132, 145, 150-151, 173
Wynne-Jones, G.V.: 95

Yewlett, George: 107
York: 84, 115, 117, 133, 135

Yorkshire (county): 7, 20, 24, 35, 36, 42, 77, 82, 84, 88, 90, 93, 98, 115-117, 124, 134
Yorkshire Cup (rugby union): 16, 19, 23, 24, 66, 93, 98, 99, 116, 118, 120

Yorkshire Rugby Union: 24, 40, 84, 86, 93, 98, 116, 142, 153
Yorkshire county rugby union team: 40, 86, 89, 129

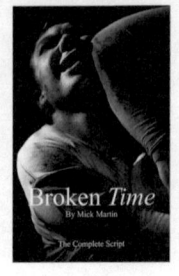

More quality rugby reading from Scratching Shed
Call 0113 225 9797

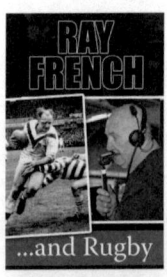

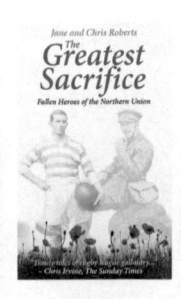

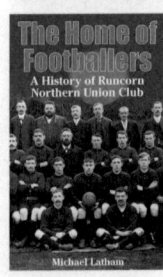

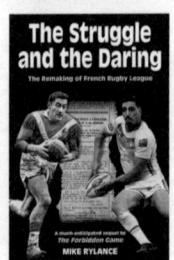

Be inspired.

Rugby League Cares presents...

13 Inspirations
The Guiding Lights of Rugby League

Edited by Tony Hannan
With a foreword by Kevin Sinfield MBE

Foreword by Kevin Sinfield MBE

With contributions from many of the leading writers and personalities in the game, **13 Inspirations** is a lively literary collection in praise of the guiding lights of rugby league.

In aid of Rugby League Cares

Available from Scratching Shed

Curtain up on Lewy Jenkins, a young Welsh rugby player lured north by the promise of money and sporting glory; the David Beckham of his day. Lewy's sweetheart, Bessie Butterworth, is a rising star of the music hall. Beautiful and flirtatious, life has taught her harsh lessons.

These are the protagonists at the centre of *Broken Time*, a critically-acclaimed play by award-winning playwright Mick Martin. Set in Victorian Yorkshire, where fictional West Broughton Rugby Club are enduring a torrid run of defeats, it is a story of Corinthian idealism and class struggle amid the Industrial Revolution and tumultuous events that led to the historic rugby league - rugby union split of 1895.

After an eye-catching tour across the North of England, the complete script of *Broken Time* is published here for the first time. This edition also contains a foreword by Mick Martin himself and a specially commissioned introduction by respected rugby historian Professor Tony Collins.

Mick Martin's
Broken Time
- The Complete Script

At the outset of a glorious and varied career, Bev Risman faced two major dilemmas.

Should he represent his ancestral homeland Wales or England, his country of birth? Ought he to play rugby league or rugby union?

Son of league icon Gus, Risman made his name in the fifteen-a-side code, playing for England and touring with the 1959 British Lions.

After initially moving to rugby league with Leigh, he enjoyed huge success at Leeds, with whom he played in the famous Watersplash Challenge Cup final.

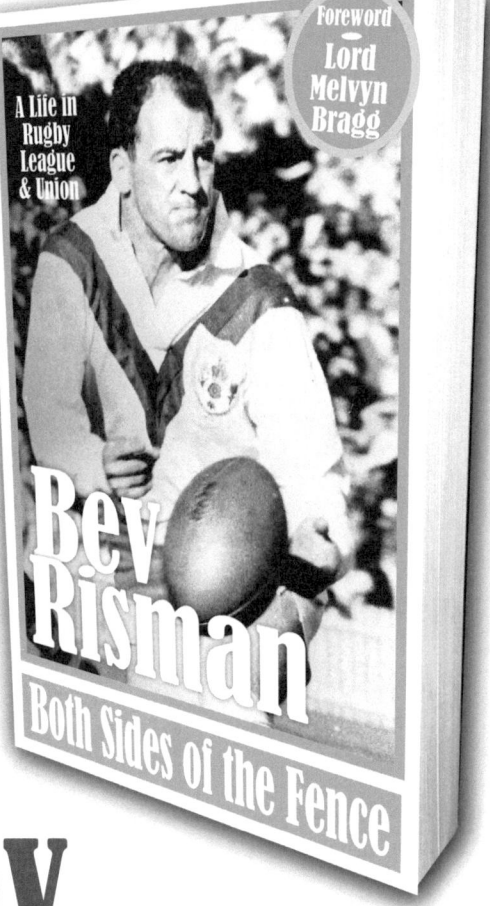

Rugby dynasty and destiny

With a foreword by Lord Melvyn Bragg, *Both Sides of the Fence* offers insight into decades of great change. A fascinating autobiography, it lays open the events and personalities that dominated both codes of rugby.

"A highly readable memoir..."
The Guardian

Investigate all our other titles and
stay up to date with our latest releases at
www.scratchingshedpublishing.com